my karma
ran over
my dogma

Lessons Learned
by a Whistle-Blowing Minister
Turned Mystic

REV. MONICA McDOWELL, MDIV

ISBN: 978-1-54995-166-4

Grateful acknowledgment is given to the following for permission to quote. Please see "Endnotes" for full citations with copyrights.

Atria Books, *The G.O.D. Experiments* by Gary E. Schwartz, Ph.D.
Daniel Ladinsky for the Penguin anthology *Love Poems from God*
Grand Central Publishing, *Only Love is Real* by Brian L. Weiss, M.D.
Inner Traditions, Bear and Co. *Meditations with Mechtild of Magdeburg* by Sue Woodruff.
New World Library, *Practicing the Power of Now* by Eckhart Tolle.
Pioneer Drama Service, Inc., *Julian* by James Janda.
Upper Room Books, *Release* by Flora Slosson Wuellner; *A Life of Total Prayer*, & *The Soul's Delight* ed. Keith Beasley-Topliffe.

For purposes of confidentiality, details about clients and their stories have been altered.

Edition No. 2

To my beloved husband—

who walked with me through the whole darn thing

&ONTENTS

There is a brokenness
out of which comes the unbroken,
a shatteredness
out of which blooms the unshatterable.
There is a sorrow
beyond all grief which leads to joy
and a fragility
out of whose depths emerges strength.
There is a hollow space
too vast for words
through which we pass with each loss,
out of whose darkness
we are sanctioned into being.

Rashani[1]

$\mathscr{I}$NTRODUCTION

$\mathscr{I}$t is no accident you have picked up this book. I believe there is a purpose behind everything and for some significant reason you are reading these words. There is a message in here for you. Maybe you're intrigued by mystical spirituality or you're already on the mystical path, and you want to learn more. Or, perhaps thus far in your life you have experienced a bunch of pieces that do not yet fit into a whole, and you are searching, searching, searching. You yearn for something that will make sense of the puzzles of your life. Or, maybe you're simply curious and open to mystery.

Whatever the reason, I do want to caution you before you read any further. The events I am going to tell you about are quite out of the ordinary. In fact, I doubt *I* would believe the entirety of my own story except that I lived it and had many witnesses who walked with me through it. Of course, some of you will know the experiences I write about are truth because you have lived through something similar in your lives. I invite you to enjoy journeying with me through the abyss and out the other side to the miraculous. Others of you, though, won't know what to think, and you might find yourselves shocked or downright offended. That's perfectly okay. I invite you to open the door and come right on in anyway.

But I will be honest. There is risk in telling you my story, not only for you, but also for me. Friends and family who supported me whole-heartedly during the first five years of the new millennium, now, upon reading the whole shebang of my saga, may decide they can no longer support me. Alas, this possibility has grieved me to my core. I am also a tad terrified that due to putting everything that happened to me in print, I will henceforth be banished to the outer limits of every reputable circle in society. I have contemplated my bedroom ceiling in the middle of many nights, wide-eyed and wide-awake, wondering what the heck I think I'm doing. However, although I'm more than a little reticent to put this book out for the public's scrutiny (I think I'd rather streak through my respectable neighborhood in broad daylight), I've learned from what I've lived through that truth is worth the risk.

The greater risk, though, is that some of you may discount what I write because of the implications for your own lives. I hope the fear of loss that comes when one's worldview is stretched beyond its comfort zone will not prevent you from considering the most spectacular of insights—insights that are worth far more than any losses you could ever experience. For the lessons that lie herein might cause you to question your own worldview to such an extent that it is painful, and thus, you will not allow for the remote possibility that what I write is truth. Not that I blame you. The risk of loss is real. Those who dare to believe me might lose not only their understanding of "the way things work," they might lose their faith communities, their jobs and careers, and even all their money. I know, because I lost all these things and more. And it has been worth it many times over in the end.

> **What would happen if one woman told the truth about her life? The world would split open.**
>
> MURIEL RUKEYSER

10

To you then, who are still reading, you are brave. I consider you a kindred spirit for being willing upon knowing the risks, to keep right on going. However, consider yourself forewarned. It gets a bit harrowing from here on out.

Monica McDowell

PART ONE:

FIVE YEARS OF HELL

*O*ne wink was all it took. With one wink the whole of my life began to change forever.

In December of 2000, I was a mere twelve days into my new position as the associate pastor of a suburban Presbyterian church in the Pacific Northwest when my supervisor, the senior minister, winked at me and began sexually harassing me. Although his sexual harassment was mild in the beginning—an occasional wink, a suggestive comment here and there—it was still very concerning. *What is going on?* kept repeating silently in my head like an alarm mantra sounding off, warning me that danger was prowling just around the corner.

The fact that my supervisor was acting like this towards me was not a good sign. Not at all. Not about him. And not about the church either. It put me on alert. Maybe there was indeed more "going on," and so I stayed at my job and tried to solve the irresistible mystery that emerged over time with many perplexing clues that didn't add up. For example, I was told numerous times that this church was "a very healthy church," but whenever I would listen to church and staff members tell me their personal stories, all I heard was suffering. Deep, unremitting pain seemed to seep through everyone in that "very healthy church," signaling to me the presence of a pervasive spiritual disease in the congregation I had yet to diagnose.

Now if I had followed "How to Deal with Sexual Harassment" protocol, I would've immediately confronted the senior minister after the first few incidents of his inappropriate behavior and told him in no uncertain terms, "Buster, you better stop it or you're in big trouble!"

But, my gut wouldn't let me. After the very first wink and suggestive comment, I had already gone into survival mode. My instinctual antennae were up and attuned to every nuance of significance and each vibe of peril, and they knew it would be highly unwise and even impetuous of me to confront the situation at that time. I had an inkling on some level of my awareness hovering just below consciousness that it was very important for me to figure out what else was "going on" first. In the end, my instincts proved right.

Studies have shown that approximately 3 out of 4 clergywomen experience sexual harassment in their career, regardless of denomination or faith affiliation.[2]

So, for any of you out there in readerland who are currently experiencing sexual harassment (or any other challenging circumstance for that matter), my best advice to you is to always seek wise counsel, be ready and willing to heed that counsel, yet trust yourself and your own intuition above all else.

Over the next six months while I sleuthed to figure out what all the mystifying clues meant for the spiritual health of the congregation, the sexual harassment escalated. Although it had started with winks and innuendos, the senior minister soon began leering at particular body parts of mine (guess which ones), and making subtle invitations suggesting we "rendezvous." By May of 2001, it had become even more serious. At one point he cornered me in his office while coming at me, acting creepy, saying creepy things: "the warmth of the embrace...the passion flower that opens in the warmth of the sun," and honest to God, changing back and forth into a couple of different personas right in front of my eyes.

Within a few weeks of this frightening incident, I heard the minister say something inadvertently that tipped me off to what the clues had been hinting at all along: it appeared he'd been sexually abusing a woman in the congregation, perhaps for a very long time. Upon confronting him, now that I suspected what else was "going on," he again turned into different personas (several this time, with different voices, postures and faces), became extremely emotionally and verbally abusive, threatened my job, and over the next few days started taking job duties away from me.

It is difficult to explain to those who haven't experienced sexual harassment how oppressive it can feel. But that is exactly what sexual harassment is all about: the power and control of one person over another. In my case, this sense of being overpowered was compounded because the senior minister had, well, shall we say, certain *gifts*. He was extraordinarily talented in the subtle (and sometimes not-so-subtle) arts of deception, seduction, and manipulation to an extent that was ominously troubling to my soul.

Like a master illusionist, he seemed to be able to make people believe him no matter what he said with just a simple wave of his hand. He was also a genius at mind games. I noticed that whenever I was in his presence, it was very difficult to think my own thoughts. After witnessing everything I did while working with this minister, I now have a much easier time understanding the hypnotic hold a charismatic cult leader can have over an individual or an entire group of people.

When my job duties started disappearing into thin air, I decided I didn't want to see the end of whatever magic trick this master of illusion was starting to play on me, so I took a quick exit stage right in an administrative leave of absence from my position. I also consulted with higher-ups in the presbytery (the overseeing judicatory body for about 40 regional churches) and they gave me my options: I could walk away, I could file a formal complaint in the presbytery that would jump-start an investigation into his behavior, or I could sue. I was told several times by higher-ups that mediation would be ineffective due to the imbalance in power that occurs in clergy sexual misconduct situations, and they could not recommend this option to me.

Even though I desperately wanted to walk away, I ended up choosing the middle route and filed a formal complaint with the presbytery. After doing so, the minister began veritable jungle warfare against me, God bless him. He defamed me by saying I was mentally unstable and had a history of employment problems. He manipulated the church leadership by controlling all the communication regarding the situation and by running the board meetings having to do with my complaint against him. He also circulated confidential documents to church members during the investigation, and in general he just plain lied to the congregation about ongoing events like there was no tomorrow or hereafter, let alone such a thing as karma.

While I was being buried beneath the rubble of this minister's wrath, other stories buried beneath the surface for a long time (decades) began to emerge. I heard from six other ministers, including two of his former best friends, who had made informal complaints with a similar pattern to mine: he set me up, he defamed me, he destroyed my ministry and then ingeniously covered it up...the presbytery did nothing. I also heard from many former church members, elders and staff who had stories with a similar ring to them, including reports about his sexual misconduct: "he embraced me in private and wouldn't let go"—"he went skinny dipping with minor boys on a mission trip without parental knowledge."

Clearly, I had stumbled into a rat's nest inhabited by a wolf in sheep's clothing who was so good at playing the part of the sheep, the only people who knew how dangerous he was were those who had been bitten by him. There was so much pain in his victims even years after they had experienced harm by him, it was obvious to me their pain came from being bitten by the canine teeth of a wolf not the bovine teeth of a sheep.

Nothing in my entire life had prepared me for this.

I grew up in a rural town in northwest Washington where the cows outnumbered the people and downtown was a two-way stop (both still true today). My parents were the epitome of small town America. Dad worked two or more jobs at a time to keep food on the table, plus volunteered as a firefighter, even rising to the heralded position of fire chief. Mom, a homemaker, supported my younger brother, sister, and me as we grew up, instilling in us traditional values of God, family, honesty, hard work, and church. Not much was remarkable about my family except how bedrock stable it was.

Moreover, the rest of my life had been blessed as well. I enjoyed college, majoring in sociology-anthropology and cross-cultural ministry, traveling the world during a couple of summer breaks, eventually graduating summa cum laude as co-valedictorian (I know, I know—so la-de-da.) At seminary I also did well academically, focusing my studies on pastoral care and counseling. In my post-graduate school jobs as a chaplain for adults with disabilities and a part-time solo pastor, I thrived, taking to the ministerial profession like a slug to Seattle's ever-saturated sidewalks. Along the way my husband and I had two beautiful children. Our families were loving and supportive. Scandal, abuse, and injustice were realities absent from our daily lives. I'd always had rewarding work experiences and good solid friendships with my co-workers and supervisors, both men and women. Sexual harassment and retaliation were the last things I expected to happen to me. So I was more than a little flummoxed by the blue-ribbon-sized pickle I found myself in.

For some reason, probably the small town innocence that stayed with me into adulthood, I allowed myself to be convinced by the higher-ups of the presbytery that the Investigating Committee would look into the entirety of the senior minister's behavior and put an end to it. Several of those in the know next to promised this to me: "Trust us. He's really going to be in trouble this time."

I was stupid-foolishly naïve. In fact, the Investigating Committee ended up not interviewing any of the former ministers, staff, elders, or members with stories. Most of my witnesses were not interviewed either. Too late, I realized why. The higher-ups had known about many if not most of the stories I had come to find out about, and over the years they hadn't done much of anything to intervene or stop the shocking abuse of this one minister. To thoroughly investigate my complaint would have meant revealing how much the higher-ups had known and how little they had done. Their own images would have been marred. Thus, I got hung out to dry. After the Investigating Committee decided not to file formal charges against the minister, I submitted an appeal based on several of their violations of presbytery policy. The presbytery denied my appeal. I was then informed I had no other recourse in the church's judicial system, and soon afterward the presbytery fired me from my job. (I'm sure you could see this coming a gazillion miles away, though I was as stunned by this turn of events as I would have been if turnips had suddenly sprouted out all of my body's orifices.) When I subsequently asked for the required permission to circulate my ministerial résumé in order to get a new church position, the presbytery denied my request. They were concerned that I'd filed a discrimination complaint with the Equal Employment Opportunity Commission. When I asked the presbytery representative why they wouldn't allow me to circulate my ministerial résumé, she tried to coerce me into dropping my EEOC complaint, telling me, "If you walk away quietly, you can have your career back."

What do you do when life blindsides you? Resolve to look on the sunny side of life as you cheerily try to convince yourself "it's not that bad, really, it's not that bad"? Rail against God about the injustice of it all? Sink into a miry pit of self-pitying introspection, promising the universe you will donate everything you own to Save the Whales, and fix every personal flaw down to the skewed shape of your belly button if only the ordeal would go away immediately? Weep morosely on your bed for hours on end? I admit I did all of the above. I cycled through the first four stages of grief over and over again, like Lance Armstrong stuck on a perpetual Tour de France, never seeming to reach the final grieving stage of acceptance. I couldn't yet see how to reconcile everything that was happening to me in a way that made sense of my belief "God is love."

What I could see, though, was the church needed some accountability, especially in light of all the retaliation against me that was typical of scapegoating-the-whistleblower. So in March 2002, a couple of months after being officially blacklisted, I overcame my innate chicken-heartedness and filed civil rights lawsuits. The presbytery again retaliated (not too surprising) and demanded I undergo a psychological evaluation. I refused because they insisted on using their own psychologist, and because they informed me they would speak to their psychologist before my examination, and again before he wrote up his formal evaluation of me. Surely, I thought, the courts would see what was going on and put a stop to the presbytery's outrageous behavior.

However, saying I ran into a bit of a snag in the courts was a lot like saying New Orleans had a bit of a plumbing problem in 2005. It seemed because of a little known clause in the First Amendment of the Constitution called "the ministerial exception," churches were exempt from employment law concerning ministers. Or, that's how the courts in our land had always interpreted it. This little clause became the bane of my existence.

Now on the one hand, the ministerial exception exists for good reason: to protect freedom of religion. It is a very good thing the state doesn't interfere and tell synagogues they have to hire a Christian minister and if they don't they are unfairly discriminating. On the other hand, does it mean a religious institution can fire a minister for any reason whatsoever and do whatever they want to that person with no legal accountability? Does it mean a religious institution can ignore all discrimination complaints made by a minister even if the complaint has nothing to do with religious belief? (As in my case—a complaint about sexual harassment and retaliation.) If these things were true, ministers have no employment civil rights and are the only group of people in the country with no job protections. It would also mean the church has absolute power over its ministers. Never a good thing, for as we all know, absolute power corrupts absolutely.

This little "ministerial exception" clause caused quite the constitutional debate in state and federal courts, which thus caused my lawsuits to go on seemingly forever. Several times my case was dismissed simply on the grounds of "church-state" as all employment cases by ministers had been up to that point in our country. (I did have one small triumph in state court when a judge allowed one of my suits to go forward. I ended up turning it down in order to appeal all of my suits together to the state appellate court.)

Fortunately, things changed when we got to the Ninth Circuit Court, perhaps because the Catholic Church sexual abuse scandals had recently surfaced in the media. During oral arguments in October of 2003, the presiding federal judge pushed the Presbyterian Church's lawyers to the edge, making them slide down the steep, slippery slope of their argumentation. (It seemed I got the Presbyterian denomination's attention—they flew out a highfalutin attorney from Pennsylvania for the event.) The presiding

23

judge asked both of the Church's attorneys separately, "Are you saying it is the Church's position that even if a clergywoman were to be raped by another minister, she should have no civil rights and the raping minister and the Church should be immune from civil liability?"

I kid you not, both attorneys independently of the other answered, "Yes."

Well, at least now I knew why I was having this little problem with the Presbyterians. Bottom line: I was their slave. In their opinion, I had absolutely no civil rights. Another minister could rape me and still they thought they had the right to do whatever they wanted to me, and my job and career, and have no civil accountability for their actions. I don't know about you, but I was *so* not okay with this.

Providentially, the Ninth Circuit Court in a landmark decision sided with my case and granted me limited but far-reaching civil rights in July 2004. It was the first time in the country an ordained minister had ever been granted employment civil rights in a federal ruling. After hearing the good news from my attorney, I was euphoric with runner's high. My grueling spiritual marathon was far from over, but I had achieved a personal victory that would carry me through to the end. The court's ruling in my favor caught the media's attention, and a number of reports and editorials were published in papers and posted on blogs around the country and beyond. It even made it into a legal book, *God vs. the Gavel*, written by Marci Hamilton and published by Cambridge Press.[3]

As you can imagine, the Church was none too happy with this ruling. Gosh, they'd be accountable for their actions like other employers if clergy had civil rights. God forbid! So, the presbytery petitioned for a rehearing of this ruling before the full Ninth Circuit Court. But in February 2005, their petition was denied. There would be no rehearing. Thus, my precedent-setting civil rights ruling stood. Soon after this, the Church and I settled out-of-court, more than three years after I had first filed suit and four and a half years after I had started working with this master illusionist of a minister.

> **Well-behaved women rarely make history.**
> LAUREL THATCHER ULRICH

However, if you think this settlement ended the retaliation against me, you would be as mistaken as thinking that wearing a red shirt in a corral full of bulls would make a favorable fashion statement. Statement—yes. Favorable—no. I was still clinking champagne glasses (filled with sparkling apple cider), red-shirtedly celebrating the end of litigation, when the you-know-what really hit the fan. The presbytery set up a meeting with me, only I wasn't notified of this until three days before the meeting (via certified mail), and oddly, the letter failed to mention where the meeting was to be held—I had to do a bit of undercover work to find out.

At this meeting with the big brass and the entire oversight committee in attendance, I was informed that within ninety days I had to fly to Illinois to undergo an intensive rehabilitative psychological evaluation lasting several days. Oh, and parenthetically, I was told I had to pay for this out of my own pocket. Fees and travel costs? Around $3000—of which they would reimburse me only up to $1000.

In the meantime they told me I was not to pray in a group of two or more people (meaning I couldn't say grace at family meals or say bedtime prayers with my children), not to give advice to anyone over the phone, internet, or in person, not to preach or teach, not to attend any church mission event…yada, yada, yada, their stipulations went on and on. Essentially, I couldn't even practice my faith. If I did any of these "thou shalt not's" or if I didn't show up for the rehabilitative evaluation, they would promptly remove me from the Presbyterian denomination. This was said to me with smiles on their faces and with the "hope that I would soon be ministering with them again."

It became clear it was finally my opportunity to bid a fond farewell! A few weeks later, I wrote a summary of what had transpired along with an explanation of my actions, and I renounced the jurisdiction of the Presbyterian Church over me. I sent the letter to all the members of the presbytery—who I (rightly) had figured were kept mostly in the dark about all the secretive goings-on against me.

Shortly thereafter, the interim executive presbyter (the head honcho of the presbytery) then wrote a letter of disinformation smearing me to all the presbytery and synod executives in the entire country (a synod is a judicatory body over several presbyteries). She also sent the letter to all the various denominational leaders that are a part of our state's association of churches. In the spirit of Christian charity, of course. (By the way, the former head honcho of the presbytery had announced his retirement right after I'd filed lawsuits and within a year had moved to Texas.) In any case, the distribution of this Blessed Letter was at long last the end of the retaliation against me, though it certainly isn't the end of the story.

> **Don't let worries kill you – let the church help.**
>
> SEEN ON READERBOARD AT
> *THE CHURCH OF THE CROSS*

A year later in 2006, the interim executive presbyter along with her husband up and moved to Texas too, as soon as her job contract was done, and not without some controversy surrounding the both of them. (Her husband was a synod executive—the head honcho over several presbyteries, including the one I had been in litigation with. Yes, the presbytery and synod head honchos in my situation were married—no conflict of interest there!) This same year, the senior minister with whom the presbytery had not done any intervention, ended up resigning amidst a declining and financially strapped congregation and moved to Albania. Which is where Lord Voldemort fled to after he lost power (not that I'm implying there's any significance to this literary coincidence...)[4]

But I guess it was Texas or Albania if you wanted to leave town!

However, if these whistle-blowing events weren't nightmarish enough, during this same time period, the rest of my life blew apart as well. We endured losses of every kind imaginable. (Make sure you keep breathing while you read through this paragraph.) My husband and I, along with several extended family members, suffered severe health crises, unemployment, and financial devastation, some of it as a result of 9/11. A few of my witnesses lived through stints in intensive care, though one of them died. We also mourned my grandfather and our dog, and we lost our home. We survived car accidents, theft, diseases, and near fatalities. And to top it all off, my husband had his very own corrupt institution to deal with in the courts. Good Lord, it was enough distress to send a person to the emergency room in catatonic shock! (Which come to think of it, I did take three trips to the ER for three different conditions during my saga—though never for shock.)

It seemed as if we were prey, surrounded on all sides by predatory energy, barraged by destructive forces far beyond our control. Again and again I found myself nearly drowning in an ocean of grief; my traumometer tipped way past full. For five long years I didn't know if we would make it physically or financially.

Nevertheless, amidst these horrific events another story and an even larger mystery began to unfold, catapulting me into a paradigm shift beyond compare. For quite awhile trying to figure out the parameters of this new paradigm only added to the mounting stress. I didn't know what the blazes was going on. I questioned my sanity—several times. But I made it through and the lessons I learned are so priceless to me, ultimately I'd feel like a spiritual Scrooge if I hoarded all of these treasures to myself. So take what you want from the events and lessons I am about to tell you and leave the rest behind. I hope and pray you too may awaken.

> **May all who say bad things to me or cause me any other harm, and those who mock and insult me have the fortune to fully awaken.**
>
> BUDDHIST SAYING

*P*ART TWO:

*S*IX STEPS TO AWAKENING

*S*tep One:

E verything is Energy

E=mc^2 (Einstein)

I n the first few months of being massacred through character assassination after I'd come forward with my concerns about the senior minister's sexual misconduct, some bizarre things started happening to my eyesight that I hadn't ever experienced before in my life. While I was attending a lecture on Christian-Muslim dialogue in the aftermath of 9/11, I noticed a light around the speaker's head, like the luminescent glow surrounding a light bulb.

What in the world is that? I mused to myself.

I thought perhaps it was just the lighting in the room or tricks my eyes were playing on me—an optical illusion, maybe? So I experimented. I squinted with one eye, then the other. I blinked rapidly. I stared. No matter what I changed about my eyes, I realized, *Yep, I'm actually seeing light around his head.* As I looked around the room, I noticed I could see light around other people's heads as well, though I could see some easier than others, and with a few I couldn't see any light at all.

As the man continued lecturing I noticed religious symbols were coming out of his head and floating upward. If he would pause in speaking, the symbols would stop. *Boy, I am really losing it,* was my first reaction to what I was seeing. I looked around the room. I didn't see symbols coming off of anyone else's head. Was I seeing images created from his thoughts? His words? I didn't have a clue.

Over time I would pay intense attention in any setting where someone was doing public speaking. Sometimes I would see light or symbols around the speaker, sometimes I wouldn't. On a couple of occasions, I saw a shimmering rose-tinted hue around a speaker's body or a velvety regal purple around a speaker's hands when gesturing.

I started to wonder if I was seeing what is commonly called "an aura." I, of course, instantly surmised this was impossible because I was a Christian minister, and a Princeton Seminary educated one, no less. Although Princeton falls into the ecumenical category of seminaries, meaning it's hospitable and open to discussion with other religions, make no doubt about it, while I was there mention of auras was strictly taboo. I knew there had never been a single discussion of such a topic in any of my classes in those hallowed halls, with the exception of someone making a derogatory remark about what was pretentiously referred to as "New Age mumbo jumbo." So, I couldn't have been seeing any such thing as *an aura*. It was unfathomable, absurd, to even *think* this is what I might be seeing.

However, I had an opportunity at one point to verify that what I was seeing had some legitimacy to it. In the spring of 2002, after being fired and blacklisted, I worked through the book, *Finding Your Own North Star*.[5] This helped me realize I had long dreamed of setting up a spiritual direction practice. Spiritual direction is a service of journeying with someone while they work out their relationship with the Divine—however they conceive the Divine. I decided if the presbytery wouldn't let me be a minister of a church, I would be a spiritual director instead and call my practice "The Sound of Many Waters."

I chose this name because in a few places in scripture it says God's voice "was like the sound of many waters." Plus, I felt "the sound of many waters" alluded to many things I liked, such as the Northwest's gorgeous Puget Sound; its Orca-inhabited waterways spotted with idyllic, rustic islands. The name also seemed Native American and somewhat Zen as well.

Generously, earning many brownie points in heaven for doing so, my husband moved his office into the other part of the basement of our house, so I could remodel his old office space with the walkout door for my new venture. Everything came together, including the furniture, to make a lovely room for clients. At a yard sale, I found a unique antique coffee table with angels detailed into the marble top. It would be appropriate for the events that would unfold in that office. (Next chapter for those stories.)

One of my first clients, "Pete," had been referred to me from another clergywoman. He called me at her recommendation and made an appointment with me for the following afternoon. The next day, after we introduced ourselves at my office door, he came in and sat down on the white, cushy sofa that was situated along a creamy taupe paneled wall. Once I'd seated myself across from him, he began telling me his story and within a few moments, I noticed a bright light around his head. However as time went on, I realized the light ended abruptly at the top of his ears. The more I looked the more I could see there wasn't any light around his ears at all. But then I noticed the light started again at the bottom of his ears and flowed diffusely down his neck and arms. I thought, *That's curious, I wonder if something's wrong with his ears,* but I said nothing to him at the time.

Later that day while I was praying and meditating, I felt strongly that I was supposed to ask Pete about his ears. So hesitantly, I called him, apologizing to him that it was not normal behavior for me to contact my clients about their ears. Then I went right ahead anyway and asked him if he was having any problems with his.

Pete fired back immediately, "Why do you want to know about my ears?"

Discreetly, not wanting to reveal I was seeing *auras* or anything decidedly woo-woo like that, I responded, "Well, I perceived some kind of block at your ears and thought you might have an earache or something."

I was not prepared for what he said to me next. His reply: "It's funny you bring that up. I've been having persistent nightmares about shooting myself through the ears..."

It was the first time I had concrete evidence that what I was "seeing" had a direct correlation to something real in a person's life. (I will let you know that Pete was also in counseling at the time and is doing very well today.)

But now I had to wonder, *How in the heck do I fit auras into Christianity? Or do I?* Then it popped into my head that medieval Christian painters (mostly monks) always painted a light around holy people's heads...a halo...an aura? Aaaah! Maybe contemplative Christianity or mystical theology would have an answer for what was happening to my eyesight. I decided to do some investigating.

In the meantime, with yet another spiritual direction client who was in a great deal of grief, I saw something else. I had her standing up to do a body prayer, a type of physical movement that can help to unblock emotions (see page 121 on what this is). Right before she began to weep, I "saw" and felt waves of tears come rolling off her body. How could I see emotions?

Curiously, what I was seeing didn't end at auras. I began "seeing" other things, too. Several times I would look outside and declare to my family, "Oh it's raining." Now, this is not such an unusual thing here in Seattle as it is often raining, or rather, drizzling.

But it was unusual in that my husband and children would then counter, "No it's not," and look at me as if I did indeed have a few screws loose and maybe a few nuts and bolts as well.

I'd look outside again and see completely dry ground but what looked like rain in the air to me. I didn't know what I was seeing. Little flicks of something I mistook as rain. A few weeks later I was sitting on the ground, on the grass actually, while my kids played at a park and I saw swirling orbs of light all over my legs. "Now what?!!" I yelled at God. God was really patient with me during the time my worldview was being overhauled. And gracious enough to answer.

A few days later I took what had become my "whistle-blower survival routine," walking down the road from my house to Starbucks for a chai latte (the nectar of the gods) and then on to a wonderful independent bookstore located nearby, Third Place Books. While browsing amidst the shelves, I picked up a book on alternative health and randomly opened to a page that just happened to mention that "orbs" are one of the first things you see when your "third eye," the intuitive mystical eye in the middle of the forehead, begins to open. The book explained these orbs over the ground and flicks in the air are the earth's energy.

Who knew you could see such things? But then it makes sense if you think about it. On a hot day you can see waves of energy coming off the pavement. If you can see heat energy, why not earth energy? I was still a long way off from understanding how any of this came together in a way that didn't deny my rational American western scientific underpinnings or my wanting to find how this fit into Christianity, if it even did. But at least I got an answer when I asked for an explanation as to what I was seeing.

I wonder, though, have you ever looked outside and thought it was raining and then realized, "Oh, no it's not." What were you seeing? I bet you can see more than you know. At the end of this chapter I'll give you a little exercise to see if you can "see" energy. Everyone I have taught this to has been able to do so, even the most skeptical.

While my old reliable worldview was being smashed into itty bitty pieces so small that any attempt to glue it back together into a semblance of solidity would have had as much success as "all the king's horses and all the king's men" had with Humpty, it seemed the nighttime was a particularly opportune time for God to knock my socks (and slippers) off. I started being able to "see" even more at night than I occasionally did during the day. Perhaps it was because the relaxation of sleep opened my "mystical third eye" or perhaps I really was losing it, but another incident regarding seeing energy gave me more assurances that at least I wasn't the only one seeing this kind of stuff.

Once in the middle of the night my daughter walked into our bedroom. I woke up to see her at the end of our bed surrounded by a couple of feet of blue light enveloping her in a large oval, up-side down egg shape. It wasn't ordinary blue, though. It was jewel blue with fine intricate lines going every which way in what I thought looked like a complex, geometrical, 3-D blueprint—some kind of an energy matrix. It was amazingly beautiful, but very "sci-fi" looking. As it appeared my daughter was perhaps sleepwalking, I told her softly, "Go back to bed." She turned around and did. To be honest, I was a little freaked out. "What was that?" I muttered as I closed my eyes tight and went back to sleep. I didn't want to see anymore of anything that night.

A couple of days later I got my answer. I opened up another alternative healing book at random at the bookstore by our house and saw an exact depiction of what I had seen around my daughter. The author described it as the "fifth layer of the auric field." Woo-woo alerts were going off in my head big time, but I couldn't dismiss that the odd things that were happening had some predictability to them. I would see things I had never seen before and then without even trying, I would pick up a book seemingly at random and get the exact explanation of what it was I had seen.

How was it possible to get such specific answers by randomly picking up books?

I wouldn't get the resolution to that burning question for a long time, but I did start to get an understanding of what I was seeing. Incredibly, the answer came from an unlikely place.

Science.

Our current scientific models of understanding are primarily based on Newtonian physics. In this model, our bodies and the material universe are machines that can be broken down into their smaller component parts. Following the Newtonian scientific revolution, along with the separation of church and state in the West a few centuries ago, the prevailing academic paradigm today is that only matter is real—only matter matters.

However, a former Princeton resident like myself, Einstein, started another revolution in the last century with his little $E=mc^2$. In general it means that everything is energy. Even matter. According to Einstein's formula, matter is just slowed down light or dense energy.

The new quantum physics bears this out. When scientists break an atom down into its subatomic parts, and then they try to nail down what these subatomic parts are made of, everything changes. It appears that all that is left is "quantum"—energy that can change depending on the intention of the scientist. If a scientist studies it to be a wave, it behaves as a wave. If a scientist studies it to be a particle, it behaves as a particle. "Quantum" appears to be pure potential, pure energy.

The implications? Our bodies when you break them down to their most basic level appear to be energy, pure and simple. This then is one very plausible explanation (to my mind anyway) as to how miraculous healings and spontaneous remissions can take place—a shift in energy can heal our bodies, sometimes even instantly.

Moreover, some high thinking scientists, Rupert Sheldrake to name one, have proposed that material life—humans, animals, and plants—have "morphogenic fields." Basically, in English, these are energy fields that surround our bodies and give the shape and form and sustenance to material life. Put even more simply, energy blueprints. Exactly the kind of thing I saw around my daughter.

Throughout the ages in all cultures there have been some who have claimed they could see such things. They have been called "seers" or "clairvoyants" or "mystics" or "yogis." Now, though, it's also scientists and scientific experiments designed to detect such energy fields have yielded amazing results.[6]

Plus, some of these scientific minds are becoming healers themselves and they use scientific study to advance their understanding of healing energies. Barbara Brennan, former NASA research scientist, is one. Adam, the teenage "scientific healer" from Vancouver, BC, is another, and his mentor is scientist, engineer, and former astronaut, Edgar Mitchell. One more to mention is Joyce Whiteley Hawkes, an internationally renowned biophysicist who became a healer after a near death experience gave her healing abilities.

Science confirmed another "seeing" episode I experienced. It happened after one of my three trips to the emergency room. An ovarian cyst had burst, sending lots of noxious fluids into my abdomen. I was sent home from the ER with "Don't worry, you feel like death warmed over because your body's trying to absorb the noxious fluids from the cyst. But follow up with a sonogram in a couple of weeks to make sure everything's fine."

> **Matter is a state of energy. Energy is a realization of the divine mind. Energy is created in a vibration of the divine mind.**
>
> HOWARD STORM
> *MY DESCENT INTO DEATH* [7]

In the intervening time at home, trying not to fret myself back into the emergency room while waiting for my sonogram appointment, I tried to do some healing work on myself. Lying down on the comfy white sofa in my home office, I put myself into a relaxed meditative state, and tried to "get in touch" with my ovary. As I was thinking about what could be wrong, I suddenly saw my ovary in my mind's eye. Coming out of the ovary, I saw different colors—red, orange, yellow, blue, white—morphing into each other and then suddenly they changed into symbols, the symbols for a female and a cross, and other symbols as well. Then just as suddenly it all disappeared.

Reflecting on it, I thought it had to do with the retaliation against me. After all, I had been formally blacklisted. I couldn't get a position in my career if I wanted to. All of my creative energy had been stomped on. Is that why my ovary burst? Is that what the symbols of different colored energy meant, that my Christian feminine productivity was blocked? It made sense to me. But I was still in for a big surprise when I went in for my sonogram.

On the screen in the sonographer's office, I saw exactly what I had seen in my mind's eye. There in vivid detail appeared the same image of my ovary with the same colors coming out of it, morphing and moving in the same way, but minus the symbols. Science had confirmed for me what I had seen in my head.

All of this reassured me immensely that what I was seeing wasn't the stuff of a medieval, pre-scientific worldview, but perhaps on the cutting edge of a new scientific worldview, a worldview where science and spirituality don't compete or contradict, but rather complement each other. I was seeing the energy fields, the light, the color, the shape, the matrix of bodies, of internal organs, even of the earth. If everything is energy, then our thoughts and feelings are energy too. Perhaps that explains the symbols I saw coming off of the speaker's head and off my own ovary, as well as the grief I saw coming off a client's body. I was symbolically seeing the energy of the thought forms the speaker was using when speaking, seeing the meaning of the blocked energy in my ovary, as well as seeing the intensity of grief my client felt signified by waves of tears.

I'm curious. Haven't you felt weird vibes around certain people? And good vibes in certain places? What were you feeling? There's not a good explanation unless you understand that everything is energy. The explanation according to "everything is energy" is that you are intuitively picking up on the energy of a person or place. Your own energy is interacting with another person's energy or the place's energy, and it is giving you information about it. Cool, huh?

This may be more than you want to swallow with just my word on it. At the end of my book, I've offered several other books for your reference, written by scientists and others who can explain this considerably more specifically and comprehensively than I can.

For myself, when I began to grasp the concept of "everything is energy," my life started to tip on its edge past the point of no return. I tried to save it, to keep it from falling off the end of my secure flat-earth way of seeing things. It was not to be. There was more mystery afoot.

Spiritual Recreation Time (SPoRT for short)

Seeing and Sensing Your Energy

In a semi-dark room hold your hands in front of you. It's best if you hold them up where the background is a plain, neutral-colored wall, especially a darkened corner in the room. Also, it works better if the sun is not coming through the windows, so closer to dusk is a good time with the shades closed or drapes drawn as well.

Hold your hands up with the palms facing you and your fingertips pointing towards each other, but not quite touching. Hold them about a foot and a half to two feet away from your eyes. Now look past your fingers, concentrating on seeing what is around the edges of your fingertips. It's a bit like looking at a 3-D holograph. Eventually, as your eyes adjust, you will see light (maybe even colored light) around your fingers. If you pull the fingers on one hand slowly away from the fingers on the other hand, you will notice that the light streams between the fingertips of your two hands and stretches like taffy.

If you don't see this at first, keep trying. You may have an easier time seeing energy around someone else's fingers. Although I can always see white light around my fingers, I have a hard time seeing colored light. However, I can generally see colored light very easily around someone else's hands.

Here's another exercise to see if you can sense your energy.

Stand with your feet shoulder-width apart. Bend your knees slightly. With your hands beginning on your hips, as you breathe in through your nose to the count of 8, raise your hands out to shoulder height. Hold your breath to a count of 8 while holding your hands up and out. Then, release your breath through your mouth to a count of 8 while lowering your hands back to your hips. Repeat this up to 7 more times. (If you have medical conditions, please consult with your doctor before holding your breath. For those advised not to hold their breath, you can still do this exercise—just skip this breathing part and move on to the next paragraph.)

Now cup your hands in front of you as if you are holding a 12-inch ball. Slowly, move your hands closer to each other, until you feel the slightest resistance in your hands or in-between your hands. This resistance is your sense of your energy. Keep moving your hands slowly in and out or back and forth like you would with a slinky or an accordion until you feel your energy. It is very subtle. Concentration helps.

Another exercise to feel your energy is to take your index finger and draw circles with it on the palm of your other hand. Then, lift your index finger off your skin about an inch but keep drawing circles with it. You will continue to feel the circle being drawn on your palm. Play with this a bit. Stop drawing the circle in midair. Notice that the sensation on your palm stops, too. Reverse the direction of the circle—the sensation on your palm reverses direction as well.

Practicing with a partner is fun, too. There are energy books listed in the Resource section that can give you more tips and tools in learning to see and sense your energy. It is not an insignificant quest to undertake, for learning about your energy can begin to revolutionize not only your worldview and health, it can help to heal the planet, too.

*S*tep Two:

*H*eaven is All Around Us
(Jesus)

*A*round the time I started to see energy, I was filing lawsuits in federal and state courts for civil rights violations. Reluctantly.

Some time later, after a long day of bemoaning my litigious fate to God, I happened upon a little book about Rosa Parks. As you probably know Rosa Parks is considered "The Mother of the Civil Rights Movement." She is well known for standing up for herself and others by insisting on sitting down. In 1955, she refused to move from her seat for white men who had entered the bus and she was subsequently arrested.

What I learned from this book, however, was that this was not unique to civil rights activists of the day. Many refused to move from their seats to protest segregation on public transportation. What is less well known and what made Rosa Parks stand out from the crowd was that she sued, albeit reluctantly, for her arrest. This lawsuit with the support of the NAACP, went to the US Supreme Court and in a landmark decision, the highest court in our country declared bus segregation illegal. This ruling was then the precursor to the Civil Rights Act of 1964 — under which my own discrimination lawsuits were filed.

Knowing it was a lawsuit that had made a difference in the African American struggle for equality made me feel a little better that I too had sued for civil rights violations.

Even though I knew the church needed accountability, I truly had not wanted to sue. It's costly, it's time consuming, not to mention a drain on one's mental energy, and in general a real hassle. Plus, I had loved the people in the church. I had loved being their pastor. It grieved me to be in litigation with them. I would have walked away several hundred times over throughout the whole ordeal if I hadn't been completely convinced that God wanted me to stay in the thing.

Needless to say, God made sure I knew I was supposed to stay in the thing.

One day I was questioning God as to why I had to sue. I mean really—why? Why was the legal part of it so necessary from God's perspective? What was it going to gain? It seemed rather severe from my own perspective. The next morning I received a devotional scripture through a daily email subscription of mine that said in summary: "The farmer knows each grain she plants. She knows how much threshing each type of grain needs to be harvested. Some types of grains need very little threshing, but some need a lot, like wheat, but the farmer knows." (The sex change for the farmer—my idea.)

In other words, some situations need more intense treatment than others in order for something productive to come out of them and God knows which ones do. My task then was just to trust and follow the continued leading of God to the best of my ability.

Still, not one to just trust, (although "I just must trust" did become a necessary mantra to help me cope over the years), I would repeatedly find myself struggling to come to grips with the litigation. One evening in particular I was wrestling with God about why the lawsuit had to be. The next morning I awoke to music as if my alarm clock had been set to a radio station. One problem, though. I didn't have an alarm clock that played music. Moreover, it sounded like a choir was singing in my head—or maybe in my bedroom—or both? I couldn't tell. It was glorious angelic singing or I presumed it was angels anyway. The words? "That all may be free. That all may be free. That all may be free." This phrase was sung several times in hauntingly beautiful melodies and harmonies and then it gradually faded away.

I sat up, rubbed my eyes, and looked around—seeing nothing. Yet another bizarre event to wonder about, but whatever the source, the message was clear. Without civil rights (even for ministers), no one is free. Thank God for Rosa Parks. Without her, I wouldn't have been able to file my civil rights litigation in the first place, let alone win a civil rights victory for clergywomen.

But contemplating the angelic choir in my bedroom, made me more suspicious than ever about other strange events that seemed to confirm the existence of disembodied spiritual beings around me. I kept running into them, or they into me. Why *me*? I mean it wasn't just a few angels singing that morning—oh no, no, no, no, it sounded like I got an entire tabernacle choir of them.

Maybe because I was still uncertain as to what to do with the few experiences I'd had up to this point that I metaphorically needed to be hit over the head with a two by four of a whole legion of angels singing to get that *this is real*. It's not that I didn't believe in angels. I was, in fact, raised in a church that did believe in them. It's just that somewhere down the line, attending an intelligent academic-oriented Christian university and then Princeton Seminary, that I (along with many other like-minded ministers) relegated talk about angels to Sunday School theology and ancient scriptural stories. I don't recall any Presbyterian ever talking to me about their encounter with angels. It went right along with seeing auras...

So while in essence I believed in angels, I didn't really figure them into everyday modern life. The mystical was not in my worldview. I had a strong faith and a close relationship with God, but really on the whole my spirituality had been normal, for lack of a better word. I would later learn that more than 78% of Americans believe in angels, according to a Gallup Poll, and the percentage keeps going up. But for some reason, even though the vast majority of people in our country believe in angels, the acceptability of talking about such things is low. I have had many friends, clients, and strangers in the years since tell me about their encounters with spiritual beings. Alas, they usually begin their story with, "You're going to think I'm crazy, but..."

I could relate to that worry. I was so afraid someone was going to think I was nuts, especially since I knew there was a senior minister running around out there declaring exactly that sentiment about me. So to whom could I talk about these strange events? No one, I thought, so I kept it all under wraps. I hid the fact that I had not only heard angels, but I was starting to see them—or see something anyway...

One of my spiritual direction clients, "Dave," had come to me because he was stuck in his relationship with God. After telling me a little of his story, it became clear to me that he was probably stuck due to unexpressed grief. His wife had committed suicide and his son had died young. Rather than express the grief fully, he had moved away from the area. Upon recently moving back after a couple of years, he was finding it hard to live his life and pray authentically to God.

As Dave gradually opened up and he started expressing his grief with intense emotion, something popped into view that I had never seen before. To his left, in my home office, there appeared two large, incredibly bright spheres of light. The whole room then expanded with energy; it seemed as though it were filled with fire—a fire that engulfed everything in the room and yet enlarged it all at the same time. Dave's weeping deepened. I started telling him things—words that were coming from my mouth, but were not coming from me, but rather through me. Words like, "Do not be afraid of the deep pain. Jesus says, 'Do not be afraid'."

I didn't know what was happening. I didn't know if the spheres of light were the souls of his deceased family members or angels or Jesus and Mary. Who knew? I then noticed that the light around Dave's head was concaved in on one side. As soon as I saw this, I felt the compulsion to go and lay my hands on his head. But I refused to do it. I kept fighting the strong, persistent urge coming from some external energy force trying to compel me to get up and go lay my hands on him. Now if I had been a Pentecostal minister, I might have gotten right up and done just that along with a command to "Be healed! Demons be gone from thee!" However, this was *far* from acceptable behavior for a Presbyterian minister.

So, in order to fight the urge, I sat on my hands— literally. As embarrassing as it is to admit now, I actually forced my hands in between the bottom of my ample thighs and the seat cushion I was sitting on and kept my hands there until I felt the urge leave. I regret it to this day. Now that I've become a healer (although not a traditional

Christian healer), I know everything would have been fine.
But at the time so many strange, unexplainable events were
surrounding me, swirling me into a spiritual landscape both
awesome and frightening, I just didn't dare act until I knew
what was going on. I needed an explanation that satisfied
that persistent western scientific rational mind of mine.
Unfortunately, I didn't get one this time around. That
would have to wait. So, I could come to only one
conclusion—I was seeing and hearing angels or spiritual
beings of a non-corporeal nature of some kind. Call them
angels, call them spirit guides, call them whatever, it's the
only conclusion I could come to, other than considering the
possibility that I was completely off my rocker.

Fortunately, though, I knew I was not the only one,
having read Martha Beck's best-selling book, *Expecting
Adam*.[8] As a Harvard PhD student, thoroughly agnostic
and rational, Martha also experienced spiritual beings that
not only spoke to her, but saved her life on more than one
occasion during her pregnancy with a Down's Syndrome
baby. She's now a monthly columnist for Oprah's
magazine. Phenomenally, she still has her credibility. It
gave me hope.

For I had been hearing them talk to me, too. It wasn't
enough to see them and hear them singing. Nope. I had to
have them talk as well.

The first episode of being talked to happened when I
was still in my job at the church. It was the day when the
senior minister creepily backed me into a corner in his
office, saying to me as he walked towards me, "the warmth
of the embrace...the passion flower that opens in the
warmth of the sun," while he had his arms wrapped around
himself acting like he was hugging someone. After a
second similar episode later in the day when he had stared

at me with what I can only call "malicious lust," I was scared. For the first time in the few months I had worked there I no longer felt physically safe. I was very concerned that the next thing on the list of the escalating pattern of his sexual harassment of me might be a sexual assault.

After his sinister lust-filled stare, I left the main office quickly and went straight down the hall to my office, closed the door, and locked it. Panicked, I fell down on my knees and said out loud in earnest, "God, you've gotta get me out of here. I'm not safe anymore. You have to get me out of here!"

The answer was immediate—in the form of a very firm, clear, audible voice that said, "Just hold on. Wait. Just a little bit longer, just hold on."

I looked around. I had no idea where that voice had just come from. It seemed the voice was coming from both inside my own head and from outside me in the room as well, just as the angelic tabernacle choir would a couple of years later. But it was the first time in my life that I had ever "heard" anything. The disembodied voice, wherever it came from, was strong, and it reassured me enough to go on working at the church.

Thankfully, the voice was right. Within a couple of weeks I discovered ample reason to be concerned about the possibility that sexual abuse had been going on for many years. After confronting him about it and his sexual harassment, and then being retaliated against for doing so, I was gone from my position in an administrative leave of absence. But physically, I had been kept safe.

A couple of years later in the midst of the litigation, I would again hear a disembodied voice tell me what to do, but this time it came with an added bonus. A presence came with it.

51

It was a year after I had sued. And a year after hearing even more stories from ministers, former church members, and staff about this senior minister's deception, manipulation, abuse, and sexual misconduct. I was walking into my kitchen one sunny afternoon when all of a sudden I felt a spinning energy of *presence* all around me like a whirlpool, and I heard a voice, not audibly this time, but more like words were being impressed upon my ears — like the whirlpool of energy was whispering strongly over and over. The words? "Call Mike. Call Mike. Call Mike."

"Mike" was a minister in the presbytery who had been sympathetic to me. He believed my story and was friends with several of the other ministers with stories. He knew there were other women with stories of the senior minister's sexual misconduct as well.

However, I hadn't spoken to him in quite a long time. It would be a risk to call him. But hey, I had been told to, so...

Mike and I met in a charming café furnished with an abundance of little round tables painted apple-red, contrasted by wooden, picnic-style fold-up chairs of espresso black. Typical of the coffee culture that has emerged in Seattle, the birthplace of Starbucks, the whooshing and hissing sounds of milk being steamed for lattes punctuated the background ambience like rubber tires randomly deflating.

At the counter, I ordered hot chamomile tea (good for calming nerves) but passed on the berry-infused pastries displayed behind the glass case, reminding myself "a moment on the lips..." After Mike placed his order, we selected a table next to a full window that fronted a busy pedestrian sidewalk. Watching how many people would glance at us through the glass and continue passing by, I found some empathy for the pastries I had just rejected.

After making awkward small talk, our discussion turned toward the issues at hand.

Mike bravely stepped into treacherous waters and asked me, "So you think the presbytery is treating you unjustly?"

"Yes." I was unsure of how to proceed. I didn't know if I could really trust Mike. I knew he believed my story but he was also a member of the committee that had voted to withhold my ministerial résumé so I couldn't get another job in a church.

"Why?" he went on when he saw I wasn't going to take it any further. "You think you should be able to get another ministerial position?"

"Yes." I decided to take a jump into those perilously churning waters myself and bring up one of many sore points. "I don't think it's right when you yourself know the presbytery didn't do a thorough investigation, and the presbytery knows the senior minister is the problem. They're scapegoating me."

"Well, Monica, it's often the one telling the truth that gets blamed," he said shrugging his shoulders. "They want you to drop your lawsuits, and then they'll let you get another church position."

"That's coercion, plain and simple, Mike. It's also considered retaliatory and against civil rights laws."

"I don't think you have civil rights, Monica."

"Regardless, why aren't they doing anything about the senior minister?" I quickly realized I wasn't going to get anywhere with Mike on my strained relationship with the presbytery. The system was blindly entrenched and it would still be another year and a half before the Ninth

Circuit Court would rule in my favor. My main concern, though, was motivating the presbytery to do an intervention with the senior minister.

"We did have a psychological examination done of him." Mike squirmed in his chair a bit, and then went on to tell me the results of that evaluation.

More than a bit shocked, feeling that I (and everyone else with a story) was completely vindicated by what he revealed to me about the psychologist's conclusions, I stammered, "But, but that means the senior minister cannot and should not be a pastor, ever!"

Mike shrugged again and said, "Yes, but there's no agreement on the oversight committee as to what to do and we don't have evidence of his past behavior."

"Well if the Investigating Committee had actually done its job, you'd have plenty of evidence. Anyway, if evidence is what you need, that's easy to get." I offered him any help I could give.

We went on to discuss getting the stories of several of the former ministers, staff, and church members in writing. After bringing up so many other people's stories, it must have triggered some guilty remorse in Mike because for the first time he shared his own experience.

"You know, Monica, I once saw the senior minister leer at a woman. She was visiting the presbytery going around speaking to various churches; she was very attractive. During her stay, I had to drive her over to the senior minister's church as she was going to speak there next. I accompanied her into his office and introduced them. I then saw him look at her. It was not a normal way a man looks at a woman. It was a leer. It made me uncomfortable. Afterward, I felt really awful I had left her alone with him."

I nodded my head knowingly. What Mike admitted to me supported not only my own claims about the senior minister's leers, but a number of other women's comments to me that the senior minister had looked at them in ways that creeped them out, and they didn't feel safe being in a room alone with him. Mike and I went on to discuss some other reports of the senior minister's sexual misconduct that had surfaced in the intervening time since I'd first filed my complaints with the presbytery.

After the meeting, I gathered a number of letters from people with stories. They were more than willing to put what had happened to them in writing. Mike, though, never followed through with the letters and the presbytery didn't intervene or remove the senior minister from office even though in my opinion, they had sufficient justification to do so simply from the psychological evaluation of him. Although alternately distressed and appalled by this at the time, I learned soon enough this kind of inaction is all too common, as the Catholic Church scandals that began to emerge at the same time revealed—churches would rather not deal with the sickness in their midst.

Yet, it had been a groundbreaking meeting and for these reasons I believe the spiritual presence had told me to call Mike: based on what Mike said, I found out my grave concerns about the senior minister had been validated by a psychologist; Mike disclosed his own story and discomfort with the minister's behavior; and the letters I gathered as a result of that meeting would still play an important role in the unfolding of events a few years later.

I began to realize these spiritual beings, whoever and whatever they were, made themselves known to me only at significant junctures. They seemed to be operating under some principle of hiddenness and would only reveal their existence when I actually needed intervening guidance. Were they members of a celestial race that prided themselves on their introversion? Were they employees of heaven's western union—they showed up to deliver a divine telegram and then disappeared into the ethers to await another urgent communiqué?

I didn't know, but I experienced a spiritual presence again at a decision-making point in the litigation. I had just won a minor ruling in state court. One of my five suits had *not* been dismissed for church-state reasons, so I was allowed to pursue this lawsuit. However, I faced a large ethical dilemma in going forward and pursuing this one lawsuit; I would have to turn over all my documents. This would mean revealing my sources and revealing the names of other survivors with stories who didn't want to be known. As a minister, I felt it would be a major breach of pastoral confidence. But even more than that, the senior minister was still in power at the church and thus, he would have access to my released documents and be able to find out who had been talking to me. It would have put many people in danger.

To me it seemed that if you knew a man had a gun, and you knew that if the man had ammunition he would use the gun to harm people, ethically it would be imperative not to give the man any ammunition. Thus, I couldn't see how I could release my documents. So, I chose to forgo pursuing this one suit and instead appeal all of my suits together to the state appellate court. This would keep the pressure on, providing a necessary check and balance to the church's absolutizing power, but I wouldn't have to divulge what I felt were necessary confidentialities in the situation.

I wasn't sure it was the right choice. Normally, I think the whole truth revealed is better than not, but being a minister put me in more ethical binds than the average Jane. After I called my attorney and communicated my final answer to her—to forgo the one for the sake of appealing all—I walked into my home office to do some required photocopying. I was still wondering if I should call my attorney back and change my decision when suddenly, I felt a spike of intense energy right behind me.

In an instant, the energy encompassed me and I became one with it. It was blissfully peaceful energy, the deep peace that "surpasses all understanding." My immediate thought was, *Oh, it's the Christ!* Now I really don't know if it was the Christ or an angel or some other spiritual being, but just as quickly as the being came, it left. I knew then deep within that I had made the right decision to let the one lawsuit go.

These beings started frequenting my life more and more. I became accustomed to waking up in the night being tapped on the cheek—or having my legs massaged—or being touched on my shoulder enough to wake me in order that I might remember the song I had just heard in my dream or the insight I had just figured out in a dream. You may be thinking, "Oh, she was just dreaming that she was touched." Well, that is exactly what I would say to myself as I would wake up. But even though by then I was wide-

> **Millions of spiritual creatures walk the earth unseen, both when we wake, and when we sleep. What if earth and heaven be to each other like more than on earth is thought?**
>
> MILTON

57

awake, I would continue to experience the tapping of my face or the massaging of my legs or the touch on my shoulder.

One night, yet another sort of being paid me a visit. During my ordeal, my parents moved and did not have the ability to keep their dog, Copper, so I took him in. He was a loving dog and I enjoyed taking him on long runs and walks. It was very therapeutic. However, he soon became ill from old age and it was apparent I was going to need to have him put down. I wanted to be with Copper when the vet did it primarily for selfish reasons. I was having so many spiritual experiences, I believed I would most likely have one when he died.

I was very wrong. It was such a sad moment watching the life end in him. After his eyes got glassy, his body stiff, and he was dead, I felt nothing mystical at all, just nauseated. With this additional loss in a series of many, many terrible losses, I resigned myself to the fact that this time I hadn't seen or heard anything to prove that any of my other spiritual experiences had validity. But, I was again wrong.

That night while I was sound asleep and lying on my stomach, I awoke when I sensed a sudden pressure on my back. I thought, *That feels like someone's forearm—or foreleg!"* As soon as I registered this thought, at once, I was fully alert, still feeling the sensation of this foreleg resting on me. Then I heard the most beautiful, deeply rich, resonantly kingly voice, a voice that could move you to weeping with just one spoken word. This voice simply said to me, "Thank you."

"You're welcome," I replied automatically with tears welling up in my eyes.

I didn't know what else to say.

I felt at the time it was Copper. He had visited me to let me know it was okay I had put him down and in fact, it was something he appreciated. Can I explain this? No. Was it actually the soul of my dog? I don't know that either but it seems like something Copper would do.

What I do know is that the spiritual realms are alive and well. They may indeed operate under a general principle of hiddenness, appearing in our lives only at crucial times — at least until we are ready and willing to accept their existence and help in our lives. I have had so many experiences with spiritual beings of some kind or other in the years since these first few, I am afraid I am taking this piece of my new worldview for granted. I hope not. I am so grateful for the healings, guidance, and blessings I have experienced because of my initiation into their worlds.

Truly heaven is all around us. The spiritual realms exist in a different dimension than us, but they are all around us. All the time.

You may or may not want to believe any of this. The only thing that's really necessary is just to be open. You don't have to have your mind made up. You can say to God, or whatever word you prefer for the Ultimate, "You know, I don't know about all of this, but if it's real, please show me in an unmistakable way."

Then, get ready and pay attention. You'll be glad you did.

SPoRT

Meet Your Angel Visualization

Visualization can be a great way to meet your angels and guides and can be a very powerful connection to Spirit. On

59

one occasion I was doing a healing meditation while listening to a CD that was guiding me through a scripted visualization. The meditation focused on the seven main energy centers in the body. Part of the way through, the speaker on the CD suggested connecting with an angel or guide. In my mind's eye, I then saw a woman in white beside me. In my mind I asked her, *What's your name?*

She replied, *Elizabeth.*

Elizabeth? I thought to myself, *I don't know anyone named Elizabeth.*

Then a thought came strongly into my head, *Look it up.*

So after the meditation was done, I looked it up in the only place I could think of—my Hebrew dictionary from seminary. It turns out Elizabeth is from the Hebrew name Elisheva, which literally means "God of seven" and is a euphemism in Hebrew of making an oath or swearing a promise. So, Elizabeth means "The God who promises." Considering that I was doing a meditation on my seven energy centers and the being I connect with has a name that means "God of seven" and "God who promises," it was a sign to me that God was promising my total health.

Here is a visualization for you to use to meet your angel or guide. You can record yourself reading this slowly and then play it back as your voice guides you through the meditation, or you can memorize the general flow of this text and guide yourself through the visualization from memory.

Lie down in a comfortable place where you won't be interrupted or disturbed. Take some deep breaths into your center releasing any stress with your out-breaths. When you feel good and relaxed, visualize white or golden light coming down all around you flowing through your head, your face, your throat. Down through your shoulders and arms and hands, fingers. Through your chest, stomach, pelvis, continuing down through your legs, feet and toes.

This light is healing. This light is protecting. This light is safe. Only whatever is for your highest and best can happen.

In your mind's eye, imagine you are going to take a trip. Choose how you will travel, by walking, by boat, by flying, by riding an animal, whatever you want. See yourself moving, taking this journey that will connect you with your angel or guide. As you are traveling, notice what's around you, the colors, the smells, the sounds, and the sensations you are feeling in your body.

After awhile you arrive at a beautiful building of your choice. It could be a house, a castle, a temple, whatever you like. As you go towards the entrance, a being, an angel or guide meets you, or someone else is there to help you.

Ask the being, "What is your name?"

Wait for the response.

Ask the being to guide you as you enter the building. You walk along with the being into the front door. Inside you are guided through rooms. Look around, see what is there. Ask your guide for information about why you are here and the purpose of each room. What are you told?

As you make your way through the building you may meet other guides, other beings, other people. All are there for a purpose, to help you and teach you. When you have been guided through to the last room in the building, you see a door. Your guide wants to help you discover what is behind that door. Behind the door is a gift for you. When you are ready you can ask your guide and God to reveal to you what you are to receive. Now open the door and see what you are being given. Receive the light, the healing, the teaching of the gift, whatever it is. Take the time to accept it into your heart.

Thank your guide and God for this gift, for leading you through your visualization. Tell them whatever you would like to say. Listen for their response. When you are ready you can say good-bye and return to yourself. Take whatever time you need. Breathe slowly, deeply. Wiggle your toes and fingers. Smile. Place your hands over your heart. When you are ready you can rise and go about your day, refreshed and renewed.

If you'd like to do more visualizations, there are CD's and tapes you can buy that will guide you through various meditations. There are many types of guided visualizations, sometimes called soul journeying—for everything from connecting to your angels to better health. An excellent resource for health is to purchase a DVD from Adam (in Resources) that shows his suggested visualizations for physical healing. There are some detailed visualizations in his books, too.

*S*tep Three:

*W*e are Spiritual Beings Having *H*uman Experiences

(Pierre Teilhard de Chardin, Scientist and Mystic)

*A*fter the Ninth Circuit Court of Appeals heard the oral arguments for my case in October 2003, my health started to go downhill—rapidly. By this time, I had been learning a little about energy healing, based on the premise that since everything is energy and so are our bodies, shifts in energy can help bodies heal. I had learned how to do some energy testing on myself, though not much more.

I was so run down physically, I was having an extremely difficult time walking up even one or two steps of a staircase without feeling like I was going to fall over and have a heart attack. I could sense with my hands that the energy center in my heart was completely stuck and murky. It was not like this before the hearings at the Ninth Circuit. I had tested all of my body's energy centers and found they were easily moveable, but suddenly the one around my heart I could barely move. Within a relatively short period of time I felt like I was dying.

Since I knew asking my family physician for a prescription of energy Drano to unclog my heart's energy center went beyond the illogical to the sublimely ridiculous, I decided instead to try a medical intuitive (someone who can intuitively give a medical diagnosis). I found one in an alternative health directory and called her.

We made an appointment for the next Saturday in December of 2003. The Thursday before I was to meet her, my clergywomen's support group had a gathering. One of the women had just had a baby we got to meet for the first time. When I picked up the baby and held her close on my chest, the baby started screaming. This was unusual. Babies typically are happy with me and she was fine with everyone else. To this day I believe it was because my heart's energies were so polluted, the infant could sense it.

The medical intuitive I chose, "Sophie," also happened to be a chiropractor, and she suggested we meet close to my home at her friend's chiropractic office. I told her nothing of what I was suffering from and gave no indication as to why I was making the appointment. When the day finally arrived, I showed up at the designated time and after entering the office, I saw her sitting inside. She looked up, invited me in, and we shook hands, introducing ourselves to each other. I sat down across from her in a stiff wooden chair set aside for clients before they get on the chiropractic table—a chair so stiff that sitting in it for any length of time would give you enough back problems to make you need that chiropractic table. In any case, Sophie was friendly and clearly French-born with a heavy French accent.

I was stunned by her first question.

"Who just walked in with you?"

"I don't know," I said. It was my first appointment ever to any kind of an intuitive, and I was in for some big surprises.

She began to describe the man she saw. Shockingly, she described the senior minister to a tee, right down to the gaping space between his front teeth. Amazed, I told her his name. She said, "What's he got to do with you?"

"I was his associate minister. He was sexually harassing me. I suspected sexual abuse as well. He's still retaliating against me."

With upturned eyebrows and a tone of voice signaling incredulity, she exclaimed, "He's a *minister?*"

"Yes."

Continuing on, she stated, "Okay then, let's get started. He has attached some kind of cord to your right shoulder and he appears to be energetically attacking your heart." She mentioned this so off-handedly, it was as if she had just remarked on a health issue as insignificant and ordinary as earwax.

Regardless of her "it's no big deal" demeanor, I'm sure I blanched to a shade whiter than George Hamilton's bleached teeth. Receiving worldview-shattering news was a frequent feature of my life back then, but I hadn't even remotely gotten used to it. However, I was so impressed she could see the problem with my heart, I admitted, "I feel like I'm dying."

She gave a slight nod and said minimally, "I'm glad you came to see me today." She then closed her eyes and looked like she'd started to silently pray or meditate.

After about 10 seconds of silence, I started to cough. This came out of nowhere. I do not normally start coughing out of the blue, but I did then. There was no tickle in my throat. I had not swallowed wrong. I was not recovering from a virus. I just started to cough. Hard. Harder than a life-long smoker would with a case of double pneumonia and emphysema combined. I was wondering in my head (again), *What is going on?*

She must have picked up that my thoughts were alarmed, because she then opened her eyes briefly, looked at me, and remarked in reference to my coughing, "Yes, he's beginning to detach."

That was it—that was the only explanation she gave me before she shuttered her eyes again and looked like she was back to praying. I could see this was going to be another one of these unusual experiences I seemed to be having in abundance.

I coughed for a bit more and then stopped. After a couple more minutes of silence, she opened her eyes and said, "Okay, he's detaching. Yes, I can see it's coming out." Her face became very distorted as she looked just to the side of my right shoulder.

"Eww. You would not believe what I am seeing. It looks like puss coming out of you. Yuck. It's not your stuff. It's his stuff, his energy. Oh my gosh." She then whistled a tone and kept it steady. "Yes, it's coming out. It's all coming out. This is good. This is very good." She whistled again while she watched and declared, "Okay, that is better. It's returning to its normal color now. I need to make sure he's detached all the way and that he's staying away from you."

She closed her eyes again and said, "Yes, he's detached. Wait. Let me make sure he's not deceiving me. Okay. He is responding to me. He is going away. He's agreeing to stay away. Good. Let me clear out the rest of your energy." She then whistled different tones and seemed pleased with what happened. "Okay, let me see what else is going on." She closed her eyes momentarily, then reopened them right away and said, "I want to see if you have past lives with him. Are you open to this?"

Not to disappoint you my readers, but I had to answer "Yes." I had only very recently come to consider that past lives might possibly be true. Nothing in my growing up years, nor the rest of my adulthood up to this sexual harassment misadventure, would have led me to this conclusion. Prior to this, my thinking was that anyone who believed in past lives was loony, like I shamefully admit I thought Shirley MacLaine was, or deluded, as I believed it was how they came up with a way to earn their way to heaven.

However, recent events had me thinking. I remembered that at one point during my brief tenure at this church, I had an insight I could not figure out. The minister and his wife were hosting a party at their house for church staff and leadership. I was in the stairwell to the downstairs looking over a large photo collage of their lives, their children, etc. One photograph caught my eye. It was a picture of the minister, his wife and their firstborn infant daughter, many years prior, probably when they were in their late 20's or early 30's. They were both very handsome people.

I looked at him in the picture, bristled at his stern, set in the face, hostile appearance, and thought, *Ohhh, it's him!* Not as in "It's an earlier version of the minister I know now" as I already knew who it was when I looked at the photo. Rather it was a flood of familiarity—an, *Ohhh, it's him!*—as if I knew him before this life, as in a pre-recognition, a kind of reverse déjà vu. I then thought, *Why did I just think that?* At the time I had no explanation.

Since then, though I had considered other possibilities, the only one that made sense is that I did know him before. But when would I have known him before? Only if I believed in the pre-existence of the soul or past lives would that be possible. But how could I—a Presbyterian minister for Christ's sake, admit to anything like that? Beliefs like that were anathema, declared heretical centuries ago. But I could think of no other rational explanation for my recognition of him, my *knowing* it was *him*.

There were other incidents with the senior minister too, that suggested that this whole situation had been planned beforehand, that he and I were both aware of this plan and had agreed to it. He said to me about a week before I confronted him about the sexual harassment and abuse, "It's time. The church is ready."

I replied while nodding my head, "Yes. It is time. I do think the church is ready." I said this even though I had no conscious idea what he and I were even talking about. The conversation seemed to come from a place deep within me (and maybe him) that *knew*.

Even before I had begun working at the church, people in the presbytery were coming up to me and saying puzzling things, like "You're the one. I know you are. You're the one who's going to get this presbytery into gear" or "You know you don't *have* to do this call." Foreshadowings, hints, and metaphors of what was coming seemed to abound. How was all this possible unless there was indeed a plan beforehand as to what was going to happen?

Pondering all of this even before I ended up sitting across from the medical intuitive who was now asking me if I was open to past lives, I had started doing my own research. I had recently read several books on past lives and past life experiences. I found them to be credible, written by people like me who had never before believed in past lives, previous to some experience or set of experiences that shifted their thinking to include at least the possibility of past lives. These books were written by licensed medical doctors, psychologists, counselors, and others with legitimate credentials and solid reputations.

Some were even agnostic scientists prior to their encounter with past lives. They all mentioned the meticulously well-documented, extensive research on past lives by a certain medical doctor at a university in Virginia.

The books were fascinating. The sheer volume of cases and the implausibility that the consistency and repetition in the wide diversity of cases were all based on fraud, made it hard *not* to believe in past lives. It was a lot like reading numerous accounts of near-death experiences. Once you've read and heard first-hand reports of several hundred of them (I have), you just start to believe it because for the most part why would anybody make it up? Most of the people only had things to lose by sharing their experiences, and the similarity between all the stories is significant statistically, if nothing else.

Even more to the point, my daughter had what I believe were spontaneous past lives experiences. One night she awoke soon after falling asleep, crying and yelling, sounding really traumatized. I ran to her bedroom to see what was wrong and then walked her out to the family room where my husband was, thinking that being in a well-lit room with us might settle her down. It didn't work. Ordinarily, I would have chalked this up to a night terror, for typical of a night terror, she was not responding at all to my efforts to calm her down. She was mostly acting like

> **It would be possible to describe everything scientifically, but it would make no sense; it would be without meaning, as if you described a Beethoven symphony as a variation of wave pressure.**
>
> ALBERT EINSTEIN

my husband and I weren't even there, when all of a sudden she started speaking in a different language and *translating* into English. My husband and I listened to her describe a number of things she could see but we could not. I didn't know what language it was, but it sounded like an African tribal language.

Just a month prior I had read the captivating book, *Children's Past Lives*, written by Carol Bowman, a mom and therapist whose own children had spontaneous past life experiences.[9] After my daughter started speaking in a different language, the thought finally dawned on me that she might be reliving a past life experience. For what was happening with my daughter, according to Bowman's book, was a perfect demonstration of xenoglossy: the spontaneous ability to speak fluently in a foreign language, often in the midst of re-experiencing past life events.

So, I did what I remembered Carol suggesting to parents in her book. I said to our daughter, "This is happening in a different body. A long time ago. You are safe now, in a new body."

Our daughter turned to me and said, "Really?"

It was the first time she had responded to anything I'd said to her. She turned back to where she had been looking before and seemed to continue watching whatever events were unfolding only to her eyes. But this time, she seemed to be contemplating the events from a more distant perspective, as if trying to see if what I had said about "this happening in a different time and place" made sense of what she was seeing. She again got very upset, and I repeated what I had said before, which seemed to settle her down. This time, I was able to walk her back to her room and put her to bed.

Uncanny, I thought, *Carol in her book talks about how common it is for children to have these spontaneous past life experiences soon after their mothers become open to the idea, kind of like a telepathic trigger. Just as with us. I read her book and within a month, my daughter has an experience.*

But it wasn't over. A half an hour later, the same thing happened again. I ran to my daughter's bedroom and once more found her acting like she was having a night terror. She then started speaking in the same foreign language and translating into English. I kept her in her bed this time and just repeated the same words to her I had before, "This is happening in a different body. This is a long time ago. You are safe now in a new body."

She looked directly at me and tentatively replied, "Okay." She then fell back asleep and didn't awaken again that night. Although she remembered these incidents for a few weeks afterward, she no longer remembers anything about them. However, I think it's safe to say that for my husband and me what happened that night shall be securely locked in our memories for the rest of our lives. It initiated us into a reality so pregnant with unlimited possibilities, it felt as though a new infant universe was born into our family that very night.

So that is why, referring back to the medical intuitive's question as to whether I was open to past lives, I took a leap of faith and answered, "Yes." Upon hearing my affirmative, though hesitant response, Sophie continued with her closed-eye meditation. After about a minute she reopened her eyes, again looking just to the side of me. She started to detail several past lives I had had with this minister, all with me as a young girl in various locations around the globe: India, South America, Mongolia,

Eskimo "Alaska." I was trying really hard not to roll my eyes and revert to a hearty round of sarcastic laughter. My curiosity soon got the better of me though, as she started to detail one past life.

Sophie said in one life he killed me when I was twelve or thirteen in a ritual sacrifice where he cut out my heart. Intriguing, to say the least, not only because I was currently having problems with my heart as he was perhaps attacking it again, but also because when I was about that age (in my current life) I was having obsessive thoughts about committing suicide. Once during this time while I was babysitting, I was fighting off the most intense temptation I'd had yet to kill myself with an overdose of over-the-counter drugs. I was lying down on the sofa and praying and praying and praying over a bible for God to save me. I fell asleep with my face on the open bible, which is where I was when the parents came home and woke me up. In typical teenager self-consciousness, I was totally mortified to have been found like this. However, a couple of weeks later, I realized I'd not had a suicidal thought since that night. I never did again either.

At the time I thought of it as God's answer to my prayer. What never made sense to me was why I was suicidal in the first place. There was some family dysfunction that might have accounted for a bit of melancholy in me, but nothing to account for such a severe and sudden onset of a suicidal tendency. Now, with this little tidbit of info that I was perhaps killed in a previous lifetime at this exact age, perhaps this suicidal impulse was my soul memory trying to replay itself in order to get worked out. My "deliverance" may have just been me passing the actual day in age of this previous life's death.

I still believe God answered my prayers in that I didn't attempt suicide. But now the possibility that the suicidal thoughts came from a past life death memory makes more sense to me as an explanation for where those out-of-nowhere suicidal thoughts came from to begin with and why they may have vanished so abruptly as well. It would also be consistent with what licensed medical psychotherapists who do past-life regression therapy have discovered: past-life traumas can manifest as phobias, obsessions, and even health issues in present-day lives and by remembering or reliving the trauma, the patients heals.

Even more astonishing, three years after sitting with Sophie, another healer told me the same exact details of former past lives I had with this minister. It was confirmation for me that Sophie's past life accounts weren't just the wild imaginings of a fraudulent charlatan. For there was no way this other healer could have been mind reading me—she elaborated with many details the first medical intuitive, Sophie, did not. Since that time, I have had other intuitive healers tell me similar things about the minister and me as well.

But continuing on with my first eyebrow-raising appointment with a medical intuitive, Sophie informed me that in many lifetimes the minister had done horrible things to me. She stopped going into details, but she flinched a lot as the scenes replayed themselves to her. At one point she gasped, looked horror-stricken and said, "Oh my God, he's evil!" To which I gave a little nod. (For the record, I don't think people are evil, but can have very damaged souls; though I understood her reaction to whatever it was she saw.)

It was then her turn to blanch. "Ohmigod, ohmigod, I've never seen anything like this. He's evil. But they

73

won't let me give him a healing. That's what he needs, you know. (I nodded again.) He needs a healing. I'm letting the angels take him. I need to explain this to you. He knows what he is doing. Most people don't. They energetically harm people unintentionally, unconsciously. But he knows exactly what he is doing to you. He is like a shaman who uses his power for evil. Hmm. But you have strong protection. You have a very strong archangel. Wow. You are being protected. Hmm."

This statement, not that I was being attacked, but that I was being protected, made me weep. I said, "I know. I've felt that protection every day."

She continued with the past life commentary. "I can see all these girls (me in past lives) coming to you. Yes, they are coming to you. Even future lives with him are going away because of what you are doing now."

"I believe I'm on the right track, that I'm following my path and doing what I'm supposed to be doing."

"Yes, you are. You're on your right path. I'm just amazed this man is a minister. How can people believe him?"

"He's a genius at deception and manipulation."

"Let me look and see." She closed her eyes and then after a few seconds reopened them, as was her pattern. "Oh, I see how he does it. He hooks people. Somehow he has the ability to know what people's deepest needs are and he hooks them by offering them something he has that appears to fill that deepest need."

"Yep that's how he does it. Anybody that gives him any benefit of the doubt he can hook." The minister had once told me how his father who had been a salesman could sell anybody anything by figuring out what motivated that person. According to this sales philosophy people were motivated by one of four core needs and by tapping into that need you could sell them anything.

The senior minister did have an uncanny ability to know people's deepest needs. He had tried to hook me in this way and I had to keep unhooking. But I was aware he was doing this with me. Church members would not be so aware. They were sheep, unable to see the wolf hooking them and selling them the bait he had to offer in order to keep them hooked. It went completely under their radar as they trusted him as their pastor and offered him the benefit of the doubt.

Sophie and I discussed a little bit more about how to protect myself from energy attacks in the future and she gave me some flower essences to take. I didn't really know if "flower essences" would help all that much, but I thanked her, telling her that I knew I had needed to find someone with *the gift*.

Most importantly, though, my heart's energy center was clear. I could move it backwards and forwards no problem at all. She definitely did for me what no medical doctor could have done under my peculiar circumstances. I believe she helped save my life.

Plus, she gave me more to ponder concerning the possibility, if not probability, of past lives and the pre-existence of the soul. My next experience with a different medical intuitive confirmed even more for me.

Even though the first medical intuitive had stopped the senior minister's energetic attack on me, my body was still deteriorating and feeling the residual effects of all the grief and stress prior to that. I was better in many ways, now that my heart's energy center was functioning again, but I was finding that my nerves were over-stimulated too easily, even from regular food. I had eliminated all stimulants from my diet: sugar, caffeine, red meat, greasy foods, yet I was still having problems.

About nine months after I had been to see Sophie, the first medical intuitive, I called up a second medical intuitive I found in the alternative directory. I asked "Mia" over the phone, "Is this something that is natural for you? Or did it develop over time?"

She replied, "Oh it's easy for me. I'm a third generation intuitive. I've been able to do this my whole life."

That's exactly what I wanted to hear. Another person with the gift who could help restore me to health. She was clear ahead of time that she wasn't a healer, just a reader, but she could make suggestions. As with the first medical intuitive, I told her nothing of what I was suffering from and gave no indication why I was making the appointment.

When the big day arrived, I drove to Mercer Island, an inhabited island in the middle of Lake Washington just east of Seattle, where she lived. I found her address without any difficulty, parked, and walked up the driveway to her modest single-story home. A teenage girl who answered the door asked me to come in and have a seat, telling me Mia would be right in. I sat down on the mocha brown sofa in the living room and waited. When Mia arrived through a doorway from somewhere else in the house, she blurted out, "Oh, you have digestive problems. You should take acidophilus."

Wow, I thought, *this **is** easy for her. She spotted my main problem as soon as she walked in the room!*

Then she asked me, "Is it okay if I burn sage?"

Knowing it was something Native Americans did, but not much more than that, I said, "Sage is good." Little did I know, I'd become a sage burner myself within a year's time.

She lit the sage and walked back and forth in front of me, waving the smudge stick while she went. As the pungent smoke began to waft around the room, she sat down in a chair beside me and pressed the play button on a boombox situated on a table beside her. Buddhist-sounding chants started to fill the air along with the incense, heightening my senses, creating a mood of meditative awareness. Mia later told me these chants were for chakra-clearing. Chakra is the Sanskrit word for "wheel" referring to the energy centers in your body that spin like wheels and bring energy from your energy fields into your physical body. It was my heart "chakra" that had been cleared by the first medical intuitive.

She then asked me to repeat my name slowly three times. So I did. "Monica McDowell, Monica McDowell, Monica McDowell."

"Okay, I've got you," she said. "This is what I'm seeing." She then charted out for me the various physical problems I was having, what the causes were, and some suggestions for healing. It was astounding. She provided incredibly accurate information about certain health issues of mine that my own husband didn't even know about. She also went into more details about my digestive problems, saying my stomach lining was shot and my colon lacked integrity and I should see a doctor right away if I noticed any changes. Additionally, she gave me some affirmations to say that would help my mind heal my body.

During this time I said very little. I didn't want to give anything away. But then it got more interesting. My appointment was for an hour, but the medical information only took about a half an hour. So then Mia went into other areas of my life.

She could see I have two beautiful children. I do. Then she added, "You have a lot of male energy around you."

I was thinking, *What?*—though I said nothing and just opened my eyes a little wider.

She elaborated, "I mean a whole lot of male energy around you. There are lots of men, one man in particular who's really out to get you."

I responded minimally, "Yes."

She continued with a great deal of passion, "They are trying to poke holes in you. They are trying to destroy you, especially the one man. He's a real SOB."

"Yes."

Just as enthusiastically, she kept the information flowing: "This is what they (I assumed "they" meant angels or guides) are telling me. You are to stand firm. Does that make sense to you? Stand firm. Do not let them get to you. Do not let them poke holes in you. Stand firm with your truth. Does that make sense to you?"

"Yes."

"Good. Now I need to ask you. People come to me from a wide diversity of faiths and beliefs and I don't want to assume anything. Do you believe you come from somewhere other than *the earthly plane?*"

By this time, after all the experiences and research I had done to date, now it was no longer a curiosity and an openness. I had come to believe in the pre-existence of the soul, if not past lives. In my research, though, I discovered these beliefs were not and are not foreign to Christianity. In fact, more than a few Christian leaders in early church history and many Christian communities and mystics since have stated their belief in these ideas. Granted most of them ended up being renounced as heretics, excommunicated by the church, or even killed (big surprise), but still the belief has survived among Christians. Even in the past century, French Catholic mystic and scientist Pierre Teilhard de Chardin stated, "We are spiritual beings having a human experience, not human beings having a spiritual experience." Recently I discovered that many Christian ministers and church members today believe in past lives, even some who attend conservative churches! They just don't dare talk about it in their faith communities. At the time, though, I thought it was rather novel that I, a Christian minister, believed in the pre-existence of the soul. But I had definitively come to believe that if we are fundamentally spiritual and therefore souls, then indeed we come from heaven to be born on earth. So to Mia's question about whether I believed I came from somewhere other than "the earthly plane," I confidently answered, "Yes."

"Good," she declared, "then you'll understand what they want me to tell you." She took a deep breath and said very emphatically, "This is it. *You* know where you come from, right? So *stand firm!* Got it?"

"Yes."

"They are showing me. You are being protected. Very strong protection. You are being protected by a strong archangel. Amazing protection."

"Yes, I know." For, it was exactly what the first medical intuitive had told me nine months prior. I had to wonder, though, why was all this hell happening to me if I was being protected? But I knew it was that age-old wisdom. I wasn't being protected from difficult things ever happening. I was being protected in the midst of the difficulties.

This kind of thing went on for quite a while, with Mia giving me even more accurate information about this minister. When the hour was up, Mia asked, "Okay, our hour's up, you're on free time now, but you have to tell me *what* is going on?"

Well, wasn't she the intuitive? Couldn't she tell me?

Apparently, she was so overwhelmed by all the messages, she couldn't make sense of so many pieces bombarding her all at once. The big picture was too big to put together quickly. So, I told her. She then recounted to me her own experience as a whistle-blower of clergy sexual misconduct and remarked that she hadn't been back to church since.

Couldn't blame her at all.

By the way, after seeing her I started taking acidophilus and my hyper-stimulation from food ceased almost immediately. I started doing some of the other things she had suggested to me as well, and later when I had a quick over-the-phone check-up with her, she said I was doing better. My nerves, however, had an up and down ride for quite awhile longer.

One night my nerves were really struggling to keep my heart going in a steady rhythm. I prayed for healing and eventually fell asleep. I woke up in the middle of the night feeling an intense heat sensation in my chest. I looked down and saw an orangish flickering flame appear over my heart area, but I felt no pain. Certain that my heart was experiencing spontaneous combustion, I prepared to meet my Maker by saying to myself, *Go towards the Light, Monica! Go towards the Light!* But the Light never appeared, and just as quickly as the flame had moved in, it also moved out. I checked my pulse. *Whew. My heart still works.* Plus, not only was it still working, it was beating much more restfully and much less erratically.

I began to experience other spontaneous healings that blew my mind (literally on one occasion). I once felt, heard, and somehow saw an explosion of light within the right side of my head followed by electrical surges down the left side of my body along with a loud droning buzz— sounding like a large swarm of bees had suddenly nested inside my right ear. *Great,* I thought, *now of all things my right brain's gone supernova.* This experience and others like it were so frighteningly weird, each time I was positive I'd contracted some unknown neurological disease and in short order I'd be paralyzed from head to toe. But no, I would always find myself better afterward, thank you very much.

A case in point. One morning after getting the kids off to school, I became so exhausted I had to go back to bed. As soon as I lay down, my whole body started to rhythmically pulsate, and I seemed to go into some kind of a half-trance, half-sleep state for a couple of hours. (Much later, a healer friend told me that this was a sign I was "moving into higher vibrations." I thought this sounded suspiciously woo-woo, but one of my lessons in this whole journey has been to learn to humbly say, "Hey, who knows?")

The next morning the same thing happened again. Only this time, I could see what I can only describe as "molten gold liquid light energy" flowing down from my head around my body. One of my internal organs that hadn't yet healed started to scream with pain and instinctively, I put my hands on my abdomen over the pain. I then saw this same golden liquid light come out of my hands, blanket the organ, and get absorbed into the organ. Immediately, the pain stopped, and I have had no more problems with this particular organ since.

All of these experiences continued to confirm for me my new belief that we are more than flesh and blood. We are energy. We are light. We are spiritual beings, souls, who are on a remarkable journey through the stars in the universe. What would change for you in your life if you started thinking of yourself as a spiritual being having a human experience rather than a human being having a spiritual experience? Maybe everything! It can be a bit mind blowing (literally in my case) to make this tectonic shift.

> **We are the projected children of the mind of God, the Spirit made flesh.**
>
> HOWARD STORM
> *MY DESCENT INTO DEATH*[10]

At the time I, too, was struggling and still a long way off from putting these events and insights into some framework that made sense of it all. But it lifted me to shift from thinking of myself as a human being having spiritual experiences to thinking of myself as a spiritual being having a human experience. It made what was happening seem more normal although for quite some time I didn't know anyone personally who had experienced anything even the least bit similar to what I was going through. I continued to keep my wonderings, my learnings, my experiences mostly to myself. I just hoped and prayed that in the end God would help me make sense of it all—and that I wouldn't lose my mind (literally or figuratively) in the process.

SPoRT

Affirmations

Positive, life-giving affirmations build on the understanding that everything is energy, even our thoughts. If you have positive, life-giving thoughts, that energy is sent through your body, to others, and to the universe. Do affirmations in a quiet place where you will not be distracted. Still your mind by focusing on your breath, a sacred word or by focusing your gaze at a candle flame or some other object that is optimal for your concentration. Repeat affirmations slowly and with feeling. If you just repeat them like a broken tape recorder without much attention or intensity, they will still help, but the more energy and emotion you put into the affirmation, the more you are energizing the thought form and the more beneficial it will be.

Some of my favorites to repeat are: I am love. I am peace. I am joy. While saying each phrase I put my heart into what I am saying. Sometimes I add visualizations, usually I do not. But feel free to experiment with what works for you.

You can make up your own affirmations for health, relationships, work, or other issues. A good overall one is repeating, "I am getting better and better every day in every way with _____ (fill in the blank).

If when you are doing affirmations you start to feel doubt, skepticism, fear or anger, don't give up, this is normal. You are beginning to find the energy blocks in your thoughts and emotions. Just notice the negative thought/feeling. Then visualize it floating away like a cloud or balloon and begin your affirmation again.

83

A really powerful time to do affirmations (or visualizations) is at bedtime before you fall asleep. Then while you sleep, the thought forms will penetrate into your subconscious where they will be very effective.

It's better to do fewer affirmations that are really powerful for you, than to do many that don't mean much. Find what works for you now and stick with them. After awhile you may need to change them so you can effect transformation at a deeper level. Affirmations work!!

*S*tep Four:

*A*sk and It is Answered
(Jesus)

I experienced "ask and it is answered" so much I became worried something was seriously wrong with me. Prior to this I had several times experienced what I believed were answers to prayer, but nothing to the extent I did during this time and continue to experience even now. No matter what question I had, I got the answer—many times instantly. Every day, several times a day.

What was inexplicable to me was that the answer came through so many different means—pretty much anyone or anything could be the instrument of an answer. And it didn't seem to matter how trivial or insignificant my question—it was answered.

For instance, one time as I walked to Third Place Books I was deep in reflection on some inner child healing issue or rather, inner *girl* healing issue. I thought to myself as I walked up to the outer door of the bookstore, *All I wanted as a girl was to be considered a princess by someone.* Within three seconds of thinking this thought, I went to open the door to the bookstore, but a man inside the store beat me to it. He opened the door, stepped forward to keep the door open for me, bowing formally as he did and said, "For you, princess."

Not knowing what to think, I said, "Thank you" and walked right in. My mouth might have been dragging on the floor. I really don't remember. I was so astonished. I mean, what are the odds?

A regular channel of well-timed answers came through my handy dandy devotional email subscription. I received synchronistic scriptures so regularly through this means it was downright flabbergasting. On one occasion, at the beginning of my coming forward with my story and complaints, the church board met and the senior minister was allowed to run the meeting. Predictably, it did not go well. If execution by hanging were still in vogue, I think I would have been strung up at high noon the next day. After hearing about all the hostile things that had been said about me at this meeting, I was ready to throw in the towel even though I had barely begun. What was the point of going forward if there was no hope they would ever believe the truth? How could any healing come from this? I went to bed that night distraught.

The next morning I got up and checked my email for my daily scripture and meditation. Boy, was I in for a surprise. This is what it said:

STICK AROUND TO SEE WHAT GOD WILL DO

> I'm overwhelmed with sorrow!
> > sunk in a swamp of despair!
> I'm like someone who goes to the garden
> > to pick cabbages and carrots and corn
> And returns empty-handed,
> > finds nothing for soup or sandwich or salad.
> There's not a decent person in sight.
> > Right-living humans are extinct.
> They're all out for one another's blood,
> > animals preying on each other.

They've all become experts in evil.
Corrupt leaders demand bribes.
The powerful rich
    make sure they get what they want.
The best and brightest are thistles.
The top of the line is crabgrass.
But no longer: It's exam time.
    Look at them slinking away in disgrace...
But me, I'm not giving up.
I'm sticking around to see what God will do.
I'm waiting for God to make things right.
    I'm counting on God to listen to me.
Don't, enemy, crow over me.
    I'm down, but I'm not out.
I'm sitting in the dark right now,
    but God is my light...
God's on my side
    and is going to get me out of this.
God'll turn on the lights and show me God's ways.
    I'll see the whole picture and how right God is.
And my enemy will see it too!
(Micah 7, *The Message*)[11]

Truly, it seemed like phenomenal divine guidance to hang in there. It so exactly expressed my thoughts and feelings, I was thunderstruck at the timing and the specificity of how it related to my situation.

On other days after I would find out the minister was spreading even more deception about me, and his manipulative tactics were again starting to get my goat (and my donkey, a few of my sheep, and a pig or two), I would receive scriptures about "prophet imposters and sex predators who preach lies claiming God sent them." Never in my life had I read devotionals quoting these kinds of biblical sentiments, but during this time, I received a plethora of scriptures like this.

Several times when things were at their worst, I received this scripture:

> But now, God says, the one who created you, the one who formed you. Do not fear, for I have saved you; I have called you by name, you are mine. When you pass through the waters, I will be with you; and through the rivers, they shall not overwhelm you; when you walk through fire you shall not be burned, and the flame shall not consume you. For I am God. You are precious in my sight, and honored and I love you. (Isaiah 43:1-4a)

I could certainly identify with "passing through the waters" and "walking through fire." I was grateful beyond words that God was making such a dogged effort on my behalf to repeatedly remind me I was being watched over with that indomitable Divine protection even the two medical intuitives couldn't help but notice and mention.

> **It's too coincidental to be accidental.**
>
> SUSY SMITH
> AS QUOTED IN
> *THE G.O.D. EXPERIMENTS*[12]

More confirmation of the significance of these synchronistic scriptures came through a clergywoman friend of mine who journeyed with me through the whole saga. Several times she received identical scriptures or similar devotional messages on the same days I did, even though she and I used different devotionals!

Other times when I was going to give up and walk away, I received scriptures stating, "Stand firm." The second medical intuitive had already relayed this message to me. I even had this message reiterated to me by a complete stranger. It happened one Sunday when I was guest speaking at a church. A visitor was in attendance from the East Coast and after the service we were chatting. Suddenly, in the middle of her sentence she stopped, looked me straight in the eyes, and said, "You know what you're supposed to do. You're supposed to stand firm. Just stand firm."

She said this very strongly while continuing to gaze in my eyes and point at me with her finger. She said it again: "That is what you're supposed to do, honey. *Stand firm!*"

I had goose bumps all over. She didn't know me from Eve, and she certainly didn't know a thing about my story or that I had asked God that very morning whether it was indeed time for me to walk away from the lawsuits. Yet here she was, a stranger, giving me a direct answer to my question to God from out of nowhere.

There were two other occasions when I was desperate for an end to the ongoing nightmare and it seemed to me the fastest way out was to leave the denomination, even if the lawsuits continued. On one of these occasions I was so fed up with the presbytery's antics, I had written out my renunciation letter—a letter that would instantly end my relationship with the Presbyterian denomination for good. I'd even signed the letter, put it an envelope, stamped and addressed the envelope and had placed it emphatically on my desk whilst I told God out loud, "If you don't do something, I'm sending this out at 5 o'clock."

Well, guess what? God did something.

Darn.

I so wanted God to not do something so I could leave the denomination. But I had to live with the disappointment. That afternoon well before 5 p.m., I received a startling phone call from a minister friend I hadn't heard from in awhile telling me he had a contact from within the denomination who was willing to help me. It seemed I was going to have to honor my agreement. God had done something all right by giving me some inside help. The only thing to do was to follow through on my end and not send out the renunciation letter—yet.

The other occasion was a year later during a time I was feeling incredibly alone standing firm as the point person under attack. The power that a corporate body has to clobber an individual is enormous. I had a nightmare during this time that an enraged elephant was stomping on me over and over. Not too hard to figure out the meaning behind that dream (sorry, Freud). The presbytery had been using all of its collective might to try to pound me into submission and their pounding was not stopping. I was receiving threats and had to read pages and pages of deception the presbytery higher ups were writing about me in their legal documents. Moreover, I felt like I was getting little political support from ministers within the denomination.

I was weeping in my bedroom angry with God, telling God, well, okay, I was actually yelling at God, "God, if you want me to stay in this, you have to give me more support from within the denomination. I don't want to be in this anymore! I'm tired of being your point person! If you want me to stay I need more support within the denomination, because I want to leave the Presbyterians! I want out! I'm getting no support..." I had completely lost my emotional equilibrium. Obviously.

The phone started ringing. There was no way I was going to answer it. The person would know I had been crying from my voice. I let it go to voice mail while continuing my barrage at God. "I'm sick of this. I'm sick of their sickness. I don't want to do this anymore..." and on and on it went. You get the point. Clearly, I'm not one of those pewsitters who thinks that prayers should be polite, meek petitions to a God who might strike you down if you're not respectful. Scripture, especially the Psalms, is chock full of people being *very* honest with God and that is what I was being. At last after a few more outbursts I was moved by my innate curiosity to see who had called. I checked the phone. Indeed, by the click...click...click, I knew there was a message. I retrieved it from voice mail.

"Hi Monica, it's Lori." ("Lori" was a Presbyterian minister from the presbytery next door to the one I was dealing with.) "You know I was just thinking, *Gosh, I don't really know Monica all that well. I'd like to get to know her better.* So I'm calling to see if you want to meet me today for coffee or lunch. Let me know."

Momentarily stunned, as if I'd been tasered through the phone's earpiece, I recalled that the phone had begun ringing before I was even done yelling at God. I had asked (well, okay, ordered) God for more support and God had responded before I was even done doing the ordering!

One of the supremely strange events that occurred during the litigation was with men who creeped me out (kind of like the senior minister—"he-who-must-not-be-named"). I was hit on more times in a few months than I was my entire life before that. I'm sure they sensed something in my energy from the whole situation that drew them to me—like a fresh kill brings out the "par-tay!" in vultures.

On Interstate 5, one particular man in a car would not stop coming up beside my car and staring at me. I'd drive faster. He'd drive faster. I'd slow down. He'd slow down. All the while, he'd keep looking over at me, gazing and gawking. More than a little unnerved, I finally got away by quickly slowing down right before an exit and getting off the freeway before he had time to do anything. I drove around the town until I knew he'd be long gone before I got back on the road.

One day after another event where a man had stalked me throughout a store I was shopping in, I was again driving down the freeway. Being followed had become rather commonplace but the experience was wearing thin fast. I was so frustrated by the men and the occasional woman who would come up and flirt or start tailing me or act rather predatory towards me that I said out loud in the car, very fervently to God, "What is this—some kind of test?" I then hit the steering wheel with the palm of my hand, adding a mimed exclamation point to my question to emphasize the extreme aggravation I was feeling, just in case God didn't clue in.

No sooner had I said and done that, I drove around a corner on I-5 and there was a very large electronic billboard flashing the words "test, test, test, test" in the form of a cross. I laughed. I guess it was definitely a "sign" that these occurrences were all a test to help me strengthen my energy boundaries with predators.

Although I continued to receive customer service help as soon as I walked into a store (something that rarely happened before—previously, I had to hunt down a clerk), over time, the creepy-men-following-me thing stopped. On one occasion after a court hearing in downtown Seattle, a man with pale, eerie eyes was staring at me as he was getting off a bus and I was waiting to board it. Even though I had looked away from him, I could see out of the corner of my eye that he was continuing to gape at me and come towards me. Spontaneously, I visually put up a white wall between him and me in my mind's eye. In an instant, he averted his gaze and simultaneously turned on his heels to go in a different direction—away from me. Clearly, my energy boundary setting worked. The testing stopped too, for thereafter, I stopped being followed by this type of men. I had apparently learned how to protect myself energetically from predators.

But back to the ongoing question of whether something was indeed wrong with me. This was, of course, the senior minister's first line of defense. I was mentally unstable. Because I'd experienced so many inexplicable things working with him, I myself had questioned my own sanity while I was employed at the church. However, once I came forward with my story and then began to hear all of the other ministers', elders', staff's, and women's stories, I no longer questioned whether I had truly witnessed everything I thought I had.

Every single freakish incident I'd experienced with that minister (even his turning back and forth into different personas) several others had also, in some form or other, experienced during their tenure with the man. Moreover, several of them had witnessed these same kinds of events with other people present. Besides, the senior minister had used the same line of defense against every one of us. We were all mentally ill. Of course, we were all people who before and after working with this minister had no employment problems whatsoever. But after we'd complained about him, suddenly we were all certifiable. Hmm.

The senior minister's defamation of me aside, though, with the accumulation of so many baffling events occurring in my life even since I had stopped working with him, I seriously questioned whether maybe he was right. Maybe mental illness was on my horizon. Perhaps all the stress was causing me to go insane. I even voiced this concern to my clergywomen support group during one of our regular monthly meetings.

Sitting in my clergy friend's contemporary-styled living room, the space framed with eclectic chairs, a modern art painting by one of her graduate students, and a spectacular view of the meandering, oceanic waters of the Puget Sound, backdropped by the craggy, snow-frosted Olympic Mountains—a serene panorama of the Pacific Northwest, I felt anything but serene inside. As my friends took turns sharing pieces of their lives: concerns and joys about jobs, children, church issues, the career-family balancing act, and infertility, my angst was more existential in nature.

When it was my turn to share, I blurted out, "Either I'm a baby mystic or I'm going crazy! Those are the only two options."

Polite chuckling from the group only confirmed for me what I thought must be their own concerns about the state of my mental health. Who could blame them? The few stories I dared to share with them were increasingly outlandish. I did not know what was happening to me — only that my life was more out of control than the Tasmanian Devil on speed and no attempts at regaining control were in the least bit successful.

A couple of days later, I was reading Dr. Christiane Northrup's informative book, *Women's Bodies, Women's Wisdom*.[13] (I highly recommend it by the way.) Dr. Northrup is a medical doctor who has also embraced alternative medicine. You may have seen one of her PBS specials on women's health. Several times in her book she refers to Caroline Myss (pronounced Mace), a friend of hers who is an astounding medical intuitive. I found the two medical intuitives I went to just as astounding. But I digress.

As I was reading Dr. Northrup's book, I began contemplating, *Gee, I wonder if Caroline Myss has written any of her own books. I wonder if I might be able to meet her someday.* I decided to walk down to the bookstore by my house to see if there were any books by her there. I went straight to the self-help section, and lo and behold, there was a book by Caroline sitting on the display shelf. Not only that, but right in front of her book was a little card that read, "Come and see Caroline this Tuesday at 7 p.m."

I knew based on this synchronicity I was supposed to be there. I bought her new book, *Sacred Contracts*, which in and of itself turned out to be a godsend, and was given a number for a place in line at her book-signing.[14]

On Tuesday evening, I showed up at Third Place Books' large common area that doubles as a community center and food court. The place was packed. I took one of the few remaining seats in a back row and watched as the space continued to fill to standing room only. A few minutes later, the chatter and bustling of those who had congregated hushed to an anticipatory silence as Caroline appeared on stage. Caroline speaks before she does her book-signings, so it's an extra chance to hear her wisdom. I do not remember much of what she said at the beginning.

I remember it was good and interesting, but I was waiting for something special.

I got it, too.

Suddenly, in the middle of her lecture, she looked out at everyone, stretched out her arm, and pointed in my general direction. She said, and I'm not joking here, "Some of you may call yourselves *a baby mystic*; you might even think you're *going crazy*. You start seeing things. You start hearing things. But you're not going crazy. It's just the wounded healer-mystic archetype coming to the fore in your life."

Hey, I got my answer! And with the same exact words I had used less than a week earlier with my clergywomen friends. I still didn't know what new worldview I was being summarily ushered into, or what the wounded healer/mystic archetype meant for me, but at least Spirit seemed to think I was sane. It was enough reassurance for me to keep on trusting the experiences and the path I was on, even though I had no idea where I was or where I was going.

> **Though many thought she had lost her wits, I knew that she had found her soul.**
>
> SPEAKING OF JULIAN OF NORWICH[15]

What would you do if a stranger came up to you with the answer to a question you asked God that morning in prayer? Perhaps, say "thanks God" and off you go happy God heard your prayer and answered it. But what would you do if you this kept happening repeatedly, several times in the span of twenty-four hours? And continued to do so, day after day, month after month, and year after year? Would you begin to question your sanity? Would you scratch your noggin' puzzling about how this could be happening? Would you wonder why God was all of a sudden seemingly paying extra special attention to *all* your thoughts and prayers? I sure did. I asked myself these questions and more. For quite a while I had no resolution to these disorienting internal deliberations of mine, except I knew I was definitely caught up in something much bigger than myself and for some reason, this situation was very important to God. So important, that apparently I needed constant, specific guidance so I wouldn't mess up whatever God wanted me to do.

Now looking back, I know I was in vastly new terrain. Up to this point in my life, I had seen serendipitous forces at work guiding my life at pivotal moments, but it was sporadic. In more recent years this kind of guidance had been increasing in frequency, but only gradually. For example, prior to the sexual harassment church, I was a part-time solo minister of a small, historic congregation in rural New Jersey. I was also the mother of two pre-school children, and I knew I only had ten hours out of my total of twenty work hours to spend on sermon preparation. So, I contracted with God that I would spend the ten hours on my sermon, but God had to help it come together in that ten. I couldn't give anymore.

Marvelously, God came through every week for nearly three years.

By Friday or Saturday, after doing all I could on my sermon, inevitably some news story would drop into my lap or someone would tell me something that would be the key to tying the whole sermon together. I found I could count on God doing this. I never felt I had to demand God answer, only that I expected it and it came. So, by this time in my life, I had experienced God's specific direction and provision on a weekly basis in a very personal way. Of course, I experienced God's provision in other general ways as well, but nothing near to the specificity and frequency I would come to know in the years of my awakening.

Considering this vastly new terrain I was in, I now think I needed continual direction, not just because God didn't want me to mess things up with the litigation, but because it was as if I had unknowingly driven into a foreign country.

If you were to accidentally drive into a foreign country with a different language, you would need a lot of help to get anywhere. You'd have to have a map and refer to it a lot. You'd need a translator and guide to help you with the language and to navigate the streets and turns so you didn't get lost. This is how Spirit functioned in my life then and continues to now, although not at the same level of intensity. Having lived a few years in this new country, I have my bearing for the most part. When I need to, I can still tune in and Spirit shows up with direction, provisions, whatever I need. But I'm not lost. I'm at home.

Yet at the time, there were still some large pieces missing in the bigger picture God was starting to show me. The next piece was a big one.

SPoRT

Sacred Reading

There are two ways I love to meditate with scripture, although it can be done with any sacred text, beloved poem, or favorite writing.

The first is called lectio divina, which in Latin means "sacred reading." Take a small portion of a text you want to focus on. Read it through slowly, gently, meditatively. You may want to read it through one or more times to let its essence sink into your soul.

After you feel that you have connected with the text, reflect on its significance to you at this time. What is it saying to you? What jumps out at you? What words or phrases have an emotional pull for you? Repeat them slowly, pondering what they mean for your life right now.

When you feel you have received a sacred message for you personally, respond in some way to what you have heard. You may want to write in your journal, paint, create a poem, take a walk repeating the words that had power for you with each step; whatever feels would be the best for you at this time.

Following your response take some time to just rest in what you have received from this reading. Lectio divina can be done in a few minutes or stretched out over a weekend retreat, but the process is the same: read, reflect, respond, rest.

Another way I meditate with scripture is to imagine myself inserted into a scriptural story. You may choose any sacred story of your own liking. Here is an example of one I have done taken from Luke 8:22-26 in the bible.

Breathe deep into your center. Get very relaxed.

Imagine that you are one of Jesus' disciples. You are standing at the edge of the Sea of Galilee, a very large lake. You are walking along the shore with Jesus and the other disciples.

Hear the waves gently lapping at the shore.

Hear the birds as they fly overhead.

Notice the smell of newly caught fish.

Ahead of you, you see an old wooden fishing boat with sails on it. You watch Jesus climb in and hear him say, "Let's go across to the other side of the lake." See the other disciples climb into the boat. Then experience yourself getting into the boat. What are you feeling? Thinking?

The boat is pushed out into the lake. Feel the boat being launched. Feel the waves move the boat under your feet. Experience the wind in your face and hair.

In the gentle rocking and lulling of the boat, by the time you have reached the middle of the lake, Jesus has fallen asleep. You feel sleepy, too.

Then suddenly, the wind increases, just a bit, but it alarms you. In just a few seconds it is fierce, sweeping across the lake, whistling in your ears, whipping you in the face.

The waves begin growing and beating against the boat, tossing the boat as if it's a toy. Feel the boat heave with each gust of wind. You are in grave danger. Feel your fear. What thoughts are racing through your mind?

You see the boat beginning to take on water, filling it. It will soon capsize.

You start shouting along with the others, "Master, master. We are perishing!" Hear yourself scream this to Jesus.

You see Jesus wake up, stand up and then you hear him say, "I rebuke you wind! I rebuke you waves!"

As soon as the words leave his mouth, all is calm, instantly. No more wind. No more waves. Notice your body. What sensations are you feeling?

Jesus turns to you. Hear him say to you, "Where is your faith?"

How do you respond to these words? What are you thinking? Feeling? Is he disappointed with you or is he encouraging you to find the place in you, the Christ in you, that contains faith in the midst of storms?

You start talking with the other disciples, "Who is this? He commands even the winds and the water and they obey him."

You're in awe and fear but you arrive safely at the other side of the lake. Experience yourself getting out of the boat. Feel the ground under your feet. What are you thinking and feeling now?

Reflect on these questions:

What does the storm represent in your life? What does the other side of the lake represent to you? Where does God want to take you in your life?

What does the Master Healer want you to learn? What does the Master Healer say to you? What do you say to the Master Healer?

Imagine what it will look like to safely arrive at the other side of the lake. Give gratitude to God for getting you there.

Monica McDowell

$\mathscr{S}$ tep Five:

$\mathscr{R}$ eality is a Unity
(Monica)

$\mathscr{M}$ y unusual experiences went beyond asking and getting immediate, specific answers. I began noticing a unity with events and my surroundings that went way beyond any previous experiences in my life. Once more, the first episode I had was when I was still working at the church.

It was Ash Wednesday morning, February 28th, 2001. I was to preach that night for the church's Ash Wednesday service. I had prepared a sermon based on a scripture passage about how catastrophes have within them the potential to help us open up all of our hearts to God and to one another. Just as I was about to email my finished sermon to the office administrator who was in an office down the hall from me, I was silently lamenting to God: *No one is going to connect with my sermon. We don't suffer social catastrophes of any kind in the Northwest, let alone one on the order that could open up any hearts. Why did I feel so strongly compelled to preach on this topic? This is completely irrelevant.*

As the saying goes: be careful what you pray for...

For at the exact moment when I hit "send" to forward my email to the office administrator with sermon attached, the earth started to move. It moved and it moved some more and I looked out the window and saw the normally straight, statuesque evergreens dancing as though they were made out of rubber and the earth rolling in fluid waves like the sea. As I dove under my desk to wait out the earthquake, my first thought was, *NEVER MIND, GOD! Forget my complaint!* I decided an irrelevant sermon on catastrophe was *much* more desirable than a relevant one after all.

As I looked out from under the desk watching the trees continue their dance and the earth its rolling, I pleaded out loud with God over and over, "Save my children, oh God, please keep my children safe." Then, in a matter of seconds it just stopped. The rolling, the shaking, the rumbling, it was all over. I ran out of my office and the church staff and I gathered for a quick prayer. I then sprinted outside, jumped in my green Volkswagen Beetle (license plate: HUMBUG), and drove the all of two blocks to the school and then pre-school to check on my kids. There was terror in my son's eyes, but everyone, everything was fine.

Back at the ranch, I surveyed my office. Only one thing had fallen over—a picture that had been sitting on a picture stand. The picture was a calligraphied scripture verse, "Be Still and Know That I Am God." Wow! Then it hit me. This verse comes from Psalm 46 that begins, "God is our refuge and strength, a very present help in trouble. Therefore we will not fear though the earth should quake, though the mountains shake in the heart of the sea..." It would be a good story for my sermon that night, Ash Wednesday, when we remember our physical mortality.

Church was full that night. The Nisqually Earthquake, as it was to be named, had shaken everyone on a lot of levels and spiritually they wanted reassurances. Preaching my already finished sermon on how "catastrophe can open our hearts to God and to one another," and "God is the one we can rely on during a total crisis" was surreal. Twilight zone chills kept running up my spine. How could I have prepared a sermon so relevant to the day's events without any conscious knowledge of what was going to happen? Later that year, after everything had blown up when I'd filed complaints of sexual misconduct and was retaliated against by the senior minister for doing so, catastrophe hit again. Extraordinarily, for the second time in a few short months, I experienced a knowing that came from a profound interconnectedness.

By Labor Day of 2001, we moved into a house in Lake Forest Park, a suburb of Seattle, and settled our kids in their new elementary school situated just behind our house. I loved being able to walk them to school, past all the towering, stately douglas firs lined up like sentries along our street. After walking them to school every morning, I would then take my whistleblower survivor routine and walk to Starbucks and then on to Third Place Books. Many days I would meander through the bookstore to find a good read and spend the better part of the morning in an oversized leather armchair, sipping my chai latte, contemplating all the while. Nothing like good old-fashioned escapism when your life is falling apart.

The next Sunday, September 9th, early in the afternoon, I was sitting in our sunroom praying and reflecting on my ongoing travails, when suddenly I was overcome by "something." An impression? A premonition? All I know is that I gasped and said out loud, "Oh no! There's not just doom for the church, there's doom for our country!" I immediately started praying, "Lord, have mercy on our country. Lord, have mercy on our country. Lord, have mercy on our country." In fact, that is about all that came out of my mouth for the next hour as I went about household chores. But it gradually faded away and I totally forgot about it.

Later in the afternoon, my husband walked up to me rather jerkily and mechanically, like a robot, and declared in monotone, "I need to go to New Jersey. I need to fly out tomorrow."

"Okay." I replied casually, "If you must, you must."

So, he went back to his office, booked a ticket online (a very expensive ticket), and started packing.

This did not strike me as unusual at all. Looking back I really don't know why I didn't question my husband's strange behavior. Usually he planned his business trips well in advance in order to get good prices on tickets, and so I could pre-plan the kids' and my schedules while he would be away. I guess it was because he sounded so certain that he had to fly, that I just shrugged my shoulders and went along with it.

I took him to the airport the next day, Monday, while the kids were in school and he called later that night to say he'd arrived safely.

The next morning I woke up hearing the phone ringing—early. Way too early for me. I slowly got out of bed, went to the bathroom, brushed my teeth, and went downstairs to find out who had called. I figured it was someone from the East Coast; probably one of my husband's business associates who didn't yet know that my husband was actually on the East Coast, and who had forgotten that we on the Pacific Coast are three hours earlier than our Atlantic cousins. I was fuming at whomever had forgotten to check the time and their brain before trying to reach us at such an ungodly hour.

Just as I got downstairs the phone rang again. I picked up the remote phone and said mildly, "Hello?"

successfully withholding my early morning, pre-chai grumps.

"Monica! I've been trying to reach you. Have you seen the news? Oh my God, there's another one! I'm watching TV right now. Go downstairs and turn on the TV! Oh my God! A plane just crashed into the World Trade Center and now another one. Oh my God! Hurry! They think it's a terrorist attack. I'm watching this live on TV!"

It was my husband. I ran down to the basement with the phone and turned on the TV. I couldn't believe what I was seeing. Airplanes crashing into skyscrapers? It looked like a scene from a movie. Maybe a bad joke. Maybe a "War of the Worlds" error, but no, it was on all the channels we got with our antenna (about 5) and it was the top news agencies reporting. This was no joke. This was no movie. I immediately flashbacked to Sunday afternoon: "There's not just doom for the church, there's doom for our country. Lord, have mercy on our country."

"Oh my God, I had a premonition on Sunday that there was doom for our country, but I completely forgot about it. Oh my God. I can't believe it."

"I've gotta go, Monica. I've got to make some more phone calls to reach some people here about meetings in light of this. I can't believe this. I'll call you later. I love you."

"Love you, too. Bye."

I sat shell-shocked for a minute or two, and then I checked the messages. My husband had left several, as had my mom. I called my mom and recounted my premonition. I also recalled while talking with my mom that my daughter had night terrors during the night after she had gone to bed. I finally let her crawl into bed with me, because she just wouldn't settle down. She kept stirring, moaning, muttering, and waking up. I had never known her to do this before. Perhaps she was on some level having a sleeping premonition as well.

As you know, the rest of the week was a bit hellish. Airports were shut down; the stock markets plummeted. In fact, this is why I believe my husband had automatedly declared on Sunday afternoon that he was flying to New Jersey the next day. On some level he too had known. With the stock markets' nose-dive, the family business went upside down, and the banks it had loans from were all in New Jersey. If my husband had been in Seattle when the World Trade Centers were attacked, he never would have made it to New Jersey with all the airports closed, and we would have lost everything.

But because he was already in New Jersey the very evening before the morning of 9/11, he could arrange face-to-face meetings with business partners and bank personnel to salvage what he could. It was a divinely appointed flight he took on 9/10. He was able to salvage enough to keep us afloat for quite a while. It was a miracle of protection. Even so, things would still be crashing down around us for a long time to come.

The experience of profound interconnectedness—of knowing without knowing what I knew—spooked me. It would happen several more times in the course of the litigation. I would often wake up in the morning "knowing" something was happening. I would feel spinning in my gut and would simply *know* the church and presbytery or the courts and the judicial system were shifting on some level. Indeed, later that day or soon afterward I would get the evidence that something significant had happened on the day my gut was spinning.

Someone would call me or I'd receive a notice that a decision had been made on that day that greatly impacted the ongoing situation.

I even started experiencing an interconnectedness with animals and nature.

One afternoon I was lying on the loveseat in our sunroom, looking out the windowed French doors at the pastoral view of many fruit trees and a mature cottage garden inherited from the previous owner of our home. Soaking in the spring sunlight flooding through the windows, I was contemplating—one of my favorite things to do to survive the onslaughts. I was deep in meditation, so it took me awhile to realize I was hearing something out of the ordinary. Squawking. Lots of it. I noticed it and then let its awareness gently drift away, out of mind and back to my meditation.

Well, okay, that's only what I intended to do. Being a novice, my mind was not focused enough to concentrate amidst the continued squawking. I finally sat up and looked to see where all the hullabaloo was coming from. And then I saw it. A blue jay was on our deck on just the other side of the French doors. More to the point, the blue jay was on our deck, looking directly at me through the doors' windowpanes, and without a doubt, the obvious source of the squawking.

Now, I had many times seen a pair of blue jays in our proliferous organic apple tree in the backyard and had often heard their intermittent squawking. This, though, was new. Certainly, never had a blue jay looked straight at me before, squawking so incessantly, like it was trying to get my attention.

I looked back at the blue jay. It continued to sustain its steady gaze at me, squawking and squawking all the while.

Clearly, something was going on and I wasn't getting it. After approximately a hundred years, it finally dawned on me. This was a visitation. But I didn't know what it meant. I thought, *Do blue jays have any significance in Pacific Native American cultures? Perhaps I should google a search and find out.* It was at this point, when I finally realized what might be happening, that the blue jay immediately stopped squawking and turned and flew away. Oh snap!

So I went to my computer and googled "blue jay and pacific northwest native cultures." I laughed aloud when I read what was on one of the websites. It informed me that in many Native cultures the blue jay was a symbol of the archetypal "trickster." The website went on to detail the blue jay as the "fool" who inadvertently brings transformation to a group. Throughout the whole whistle-blowing saga I had often referred to myself as the archetypal Stupid Fool. Clearly, the universe was confirming this for me. Even though the situation was way beyond my comprehension, somehow through my cluelessness, I was inadvertently acting as a catalyst for systemic transformation.

After that day, blue jays continued to show up frequently during my saga (one just showed up now). They would often fly right in front of me when I was in the car or on a walk, squawking all the while especially at poignant moments. For example, after my saga was fait accompli, in the fall of 2005 I received a survey for clergy in the mail from the Presbyterian denomination. Clearly the larger system had not yet been informed that I had left their fold. However, before I received this survey, I had been wondering how I could "talk back" to the larger system about everything that had happened. Thus, I was pleasantly surprised, if not greatly humored, to find that at the end of the survey I was invited to freely write any comments I wanted to about my opinion of the Presbyterian Church.

I decided it was not an accident that I had received this survey! None of my clergy friends I checked with had received it. My intuition was soon confirmed. As I sat at my desk filling out the survey, I looked up and out my office window that overlooks our backyard. Just at that moment, a blue jay flew right in front of the window and squawked. I laughed. Indeed another opportunity to be a Stupid Fool and hopefully a catalyst for more systemic transformation as well. At the very least, it certainly felt great to get to communicate to the larger church some things I saw that were broken and unjust in the system.

Other animals figured in at other times. An injured raccoon showed up on my doorstep in the middle of the day, a startling symbol of how I felt—wounded and out of sync with my community and natural rhythms. When I was going through rapid periods of physical healing, butterflies would fly all around me. After the situation was over and I saw blue jays less and less, a pair of doves started frequenting my path for the first time in my life—the consummate symbol of peace. I couldn't believe the incredible interconnectedness and unity I experienced with nature.

> **A vast similitude interlocks all.**
>
> WALT WHITMAN

Even with ice.

Because of the bucket loads of stress my husband and I were dealing with, we both suffered significant "issues in our tissues" as I have mentioned. For myself, I suffered debilitating nerve damage. Literally, my nerves were fried.

I could even hear my nerve endings fraying inside my body. One of the symptoms of this was that I had a very difficult time falling asleep as my nerves wouldn't settle down and allow me to transition into rest. Sometimes my heart's nerves would actually spark. When my cat would lie on my chest during this time, she would yelp because the nerves' sparks hurt her so much, though she'd sacrificially stay put on my chest. The nights she'd do this, I would fall asleep much easier and faster. God bless my cat, Marbles.

Around this time, I was reading in Donna Eden's book, *Energy Medicine*, about magnetic poles and how different people are helped by finding what compass direction is their strongest position in which to sleep.[16] I thought this was interesting but I didn't apply the information to my own situation.

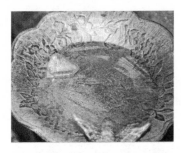

A few weeks later during a winter chill, the water in a birdbath that sat outside my home office froze solid. Nothing unusual here. I've found water generally freezes when the temperature dips below 32°F. However, when I went outside I noticed something odd about the ice. I looked closer. In the middle of the ice, there was a protrusion sticking up about an inch and a half, and the protrusion was frozen in the shape of a triangle

This was peculiar. The ice in the birdbath had never formed anything before, except cracks. This, however, was a perfectly shaped triangle. It definitely got my attention. I called my husband and kids and then took a couple of photos. I wondered, *Does it mean something?* I knew not to dismiss the possible significance. Too many uncanny things were happening all around me to do that.

As I pondered the triangle, I noticed that it looked more like an arrow. It was not an equilateral triangle e, but an elongated triangle (an isosceles triangle to be precise) and the main point was pointing due north. *Does that mean something too?*

Then the Donna Eden material I had read about magnetic poles popped into my head. Was there a connection? I did some energy muscle tests (kinesiology) and discovered due north was my optimal direction to sleep in. I then convinced my husband that the ice triangle was an arrow telling me to redirect the direction of our bed so our heads were pointing north.

Well okay, I didn't really convince him of that. I just persuaded him to move the bed as an experiment. Amazingly, we both started sleeping better and I had an easier time falling asleep as well. By the way, the birdbath has never formed any type of ice protrusion in the years since.

Beyond experiencing a oneness with the external material world all around me, I started experiencing an internal interconnectedness with reality through my so-called mystical third eye situated between the eyebrows. On several occasions in the middle of the night I would get up to visit the bathroom, a routine that began during my first pregnancy and has continued to the present day even though I have been done gestating for over a decade now—

one of the many side benefits of having one's body taken over by another being. Anyway, as I would make my way back to my bed all of a sudden a "tunnel" would appear in my vision and then a sort of a visual porthole would pop into view.

At the time, I didn't know it was my mystical third eye opening, but it seemed as though a film projector in my head had suddenly switched on and was projecting a movie onto an invisible screen about five feet in front of me. I started being able to see people in different places: once I watched a group of people milling around what looked like a game table or maybe a gambling table; another time I saw a person hiding scrolls in a golden temple; and sometimes I saw random images like flags and geometric shapes that were colorfully detailed and awesomely designed.

On occasion I even felt drawn into these places, like I was being pulled or sucked into the visual tunnel, which I heartily resisted with all my might. I'd quickly jump back into bed, squeeze my eyes tightly closed, and wonder if parallel universes and other inhabited planets might be an actual possibility. I decided I did not want to know and if there were aliens they had better leave me alone because I would put up a fight. Fortunately, an alien abduction is not part of my story. Thank God. I don't know how I would have integrated that into my life.

But that's not all. Yep. If messages in ice formations and visual portholes into the universe ain't far out enough for you, I've got more where that came from.

Elevator music. Yessiree. I even experienced interconnectedness with elevator music.

One day I received an email devotional that talked about how sometimes we can be called to be like a tugboat.

A tugboat, even though very small in comparison to a great ship can, nevertheless, get that great ship back on course by pushing on it a little bit over a long time. In addition to this, many times people had remarked to me that the church was like the Titanic—a great ship but with serious fatal flaws if it didn't heed the warnings and turn around in time. This is one of the messages that repeatedly showed up throughout my arduous waiting for the litigation to end: I was a tugboat to the Titanic.

Lucky me.

A few days later, while doing errands in a store I was asking God in my head, *Why is this taking so long? Really, can it be so hard for You to have this whole ordeal over with so I can be done with it all?*

As soon as I finished saying this, the store's background music started playing Amy Grant's song, "It takes a little time sometimes, to turn the Titanic around. But baby you're not going down. It takes more than you got right now. But baby, give it time."[17]

This musical synchronicity happened a few more times in the months and years ahead. I'd be thinking, *Gosh, this is taking so long,* and on the radio or in the store, this same Amy Grant song would start playing.

Who knew God was in elevator music, too? But all the same it was a good message. As you know, everyone was in denial about the Titanic, the fated grand ship that sank after hitting an iceberg. Even after it hit the iceberg no one wanted to believe it could go down. It was the unsinkable ship after all. But there were major design flaws in its underbelly that had been overlooked. So it is with the Presbyterian Church and perhaps the institutional church in general in our country. I know. I've been in the underbelly of that whale of a ship and I've seen the systemic faults.

They're big enough to sink it. Has the institutional church already hit the iceberg? Is it too late to turn it around?

Only God knows. All I know is I was called to be a tugboat for five long years. From the looks of where things stand right now, I'm not sure how much good it did for anyone, except for clergy who experience sexual harassment, which is plenty good enough. But with the unprecedented ruling of the Ninth Circuit Court providing new accountability and a necessary check and balance on what has been the church's absolute power over its ministers, perhaps other churches will be able to stay afloat by learning the lessons from this ruling, even if it's too late for this particular church or denomination.

As we all know, absolute power corrupts absolutely. It is similar to the *Lord of the Rings* symbology. The Ring stood for unaccountable power, absolute power. This is what evil actions are rooted in. The church in wanting absolutely no external involvement by society to look at any churchly affairs is naïve about the lure, the power of the Ring. Even the purest of hearts and the best of systems it will corrupt over time. Absolute power must be put to an end in order for the evil in our own hearts, families, churches, institutions, and country to be uprooted, transformed, and healed.

> **There never was much hope...just a fool's hope.**
>
> GANDALF
> *THE LORD OF THE RINGS*[18]

Remarkably, the *Lord of the Rings* movies were released the three Decembers my civil rights lawsuits with the Church were in effect: 2002, 2003, 2004. These were also the years that the Catholic Church sexual abuse scandals broke into the public eye. Moreover, it was on April Fools' Day of 2005, (remember the significance of

116

the blue jays?) when I settled out of court with the church. These synchronicities with current events, movies (the movie *Whale Rider* was another noteworthy one), books (the Harry Potter series), and the timing of days show even more of the profound interconnectedness I experienced throughout this period.

Because of the radical unity I was experiencing through pretty much anyone or anything, I was having a difficult time processing how all of it was even possible let alone why it was happening to me. As I have said, I was clearly in the midst of a rebirthing, a time of transition into a larger worldview. During this time I had the impression that I was collecting pieces of a puzzle that would someday (hopefully) fit into a larger picture. The Caroline Myss "baby mystic" piece was a big one. Although I didn't yet understand what was happening, I at least was given reassurances I was on the right path.

But my mind was chaos. How can God be everywhere at once? How can I be experiencing God giving me guidance through animals that appear on my deck and doorstep, let alone through elevator music, and an ice protrusion that literally pointed me in the right direction? I mean, you name it—God spoke to me through it. How in the world was that possible?

I know I should have just chalked it up to mystery and been satisfied, but I wasn't. I wanted an explanation. These things did not occur like this in the past to me, and it certainly didn't fit my understanding of *the way things worked*. Having read the aforementioned book, *Expecting Adam*, and therefore, knowing someone else had been as mystified by the events in her life as I was in mine, was more reassurance, but I still wanted to know *how* it was possible. I kept praying for a "mental map." I needed a tool, some device to help me process what kept happening (to my utter astonishment) day after day in this new terrain.

When I would pray for this "mental map" I would see a geometric figure in my mind's eye. This figure consisted of several concentric circles with an equal-sided cross superimposed over the circles (see insert). This was not

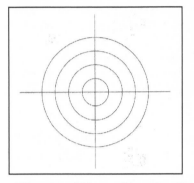

helpful at all, which I told God, because it meant absolutely nothing to me.

Until, that is, I was ambling through the bookstore by my house (again) and randomly picked up a book on one of the display shelves in the philosophy section called, *A Theory of Everything*, by Ken Wilber.[19] I opened the book and on the page I randomly opened to, there was this same geometric figure I kept seeing visually when I would pray for a mental map. Ken Wilber called it a paradigm of an integral vision that posits science and spirituality together in a unified worldview. He even referred to his paradigm as *a **mental map*** of the kosmos! Needless to say, I sat down right there and read the book *in toto*.

It provided me with exactly the tool I needed to process much of what had been happening. There is no way I can describe in a small space Wilber's entire philosophical theory, but it is enough to say that he views Spirit as present in all places in all ways at all times. We, on the other hand, look through limited lenses or worldviews. As we grow, we transition into larger and larger worldviews that help us to see through larger and more integral lenses. Communities and countries too, can grow through these worldviews, though at any one time there will be varying percentages of the people in each of the worldviews.

The concentric circles then represent the larger and larger worldviews we grow into and the equal-sided cross divides the circles into quadrants representing subjective and objective knowledge as well as individuated and communal or systemic knowledge: I, we, it and its. But in and through it all Spirit is present. This is a *very* brief explanation of his extremely complex, well thought out and yet elegantly simple paradigm, but it gives you a flavor.

It helped me immensely. Now I finally had a framework for seeing Spirit in all. It was a way of conceptualizing the radical unity I continually experienced. I could also use this framework to analyze the church's way of doing things. They could see the events at hand only through their worldview, which appeared to be smaller than mine. This did not make me superior. I had been in their worldview at some point in my life. If I were still there, I might be making the same decisions and taking the same actions they were. This did not mean they

> **For my part, when I gained the unshakable belief that there is no death, that all life is indivisible, that the here and the hereafter are one, that time and eternity are inseparable, that this is one unobstructed universe, then I found the most satisfying and convincing philosophy of my entire life.**
>
> NORMAN VINCENT PEALE
> *THE POWER OF POSITIVE THINKING*[20]

were right. It meant they had a point, but that they were seeing things from a limited perspective that did not take into mind the bigger picture and therefore lacked insight. It also helped me understand in part the senior minister's way of doing things. He was probably at an even smaller worldview still. Unfortunately, though, when someone persists at a small worldview into adulthood, things tend to get skewed and off-balance. For example, adults who have a very limited view of the world (extremely ego-centered) and yet who run large corporations (or churches) might be very good at manipulating a lot of power for a time. However, it can eventually blow up in their faces, as they are not assessing all of the factors that a larger, more integral worldview would take into account. Think Enron.

This radical unity and interconnectedness of Spirit was also a more comprehensive and complementary way of understanding the scientific theory of a holographic universe. In any film hologram, let's say it's of a basketball, if the film is divided into pieces, the original image of the entire basketball can still be created from even one of the film's pieces. The whole is contained in any part. This is how many brilliant scientists see the entire universe functioning. (For more reading on this check out the Resources section.)

It goes hand and hand with Wilber's philosophical idea of an interconnected unity under-girding all of reality. Scientific experiments regarding this holographic model have been very successful giving possible explanations to many unexplainable scientific phenomena as well as to mystical, psychic, and so-called paranormal phenomena. It also gave me more solid footing for everything I was experiencing.

This concept of an integral worldview, of a radical oneness, a radical unity of all of reality, was a huge piece in the bigger picture that was slowly coming together. It would be the next piece though, that would bring everything into focus and provide me with a healing, a far deeper healing, than I ever could have imagined.

SPoRT

Body Prayer

Body prayer is an excellent way of engaging your whole self in prayer. If we keep in mind the idea of a holographic universe where the whole is in every part, then working with your body in prayer helps every part of your body and it helps every part of the universe. You can take any poem, prayer, psalm, song, or sacred text and make up your own body motions that go along with the words. This is a very powerful way to pray, especially when your emotions are locked up. It can help to release whatever is keeping you from grieving or getting in touch with what is really going on inside you and your thoughts, feelings and body.

This is one of my favorite poems to do as body prayer. Make up body motions to each phrase that connect you to the meaning of the words. Then say the prayer out loud as you simultaneously express the prayer with your body.

In the full mystery of this hour
deeper than hearing, vaster than sight,
wrapped in your nearness, lifted in power,
Beloved, I drink your healing light . . .

Into my heart a radiant sun,
a sea of shining water flows.
Each thirsting cell, filled one by one,
within, throughout, my body glows.

Poured from the glory of your gaze,
immortal waves of love released,
renewed within your heart's bright blaze,
were never born, have never ceased.

This hour is gathered into your hands;
deep in your peace my body lies;
strong in your strength my joy stands;
borne on your wings my spirit flies

Into that sun that rings me round,
lightness of light, and glowing flame,
into your sea that does not drown,
into your heart that calls my name.

Gloria, Love, supreme, undying,
Gloria, Jesus, dear desire,
Gloria, Spirit, swift wings flying,
bringing the comfort, bringing the fire.[21]

Try this SPoRT with your favorite prayers, poems or songs. If you have or know children, enlist their help. They're naturally good at praying with their whole bodies.

$\mathscr{S}$tep Six:

$\mathscr{F}$inally Getting The Biggest Joke in the Universe

$\mathscr{P}$iece by piece over time, I was getting glimpses of a larger picture, a much bigger worldview than my previous one. But I had to piece the pieces together without knowing what the larger picture was going to be. If you've ever tried to put a complex jigsaw puzzle together without first knowing what the picture was, you know how exasperating and bewildering an experience this is.

Part of the difficulty was knowing that if I described to someone else everything that was happening to me, I was afraid they would think I had a messiah complex or something far worse. So I kept much of it to myself and only let out small bits and pieces to different people I trusted. However, I knew I wasn't *the* messiah, although my story did have a "Christ figure" or "Christ path" theme to it. In fact, it was my knowledge that I wasn't *the* messiah that put a stumbling block in the way of my understanding.

Conceivably, if all of these miraculous events were happening to me in such an astounding amount, then it would follow that these events could be happening to everyone else all the time as well. This obliterated my old worldview. I could see God getting messages through to everyone on occasion through a few tried and true practices (prayer, scripture) but to everyone all the time through any means?

The "reality is a unity" piece of the puzzle did help tremendously. All of these things could happen simultaneously everywhere because Spirit was present in all. Seeing everything as a radical unity helped explain the universe's specific answering of my questions through all sorts of avenues all the time. But for some reason, I didn't yet understand the larger implications of what this meant for me personally. The "reality is a unity" piece still didn't heal me. I needed one more piece for that.

As I was struggling with what the blasted big picture was, I was also trying to find sanctuary in the midst of all the retaliation against me. A pastor friend of mine suggested I meet a pastor friend of his named "John" and said John's church would be a safe place to worship. It truly was and John himself was very hospitable. I ended up worshiping there for the next two and a half years, occasionally preaching and teaching, and doing spiritual direction. When I met John, he suggested that because of my contemplative interests I should meet with a pastor friend of his named "Phil."

I took his suggestion as perhaps another divine hint and called Phil. But after talking with Phil over the phone, I didn't know if I wanted to meet with him. His voice sounded just like the senior minister's who had sexually harassed me. Yikes! However, I decided to trust the steps I was being shown and determined I could always end the meeting or be very discreet with the information I would give out to make sure I was safe. This meeting, though, turned out to be Doctor God's perfect prescription for me.

Phil recommended we meet for lunch at an urban truck stop famous for its sandwiches. We met there at a quarter to noon to avoid the lunchtime rush. Smart move. By the time the minute hand on the clock was five minutes past straight up, the diner was full with a long line of customers snaking from the order counter all the way out the door to the sidewalk. Though the sandwich I ordered lived up to the diner's reputation, the interior design of the eatery left much to be desired.

The booth Phil and I sat in was stiffly contoured and made of upholstered, ketchup-red plastic. The table you ask? A particularly eye-straining shade of mustard yellow Formica, making the place look like Ronald McDonald himself had donated the decor. The concrete floors only added to the "we aren't about frills" interior design theme the owners apparently thought would appeal to truck drivers, while hoping the food itself would lure a larger crowd. Their strategy seemed to be working.

As the number of people inside the restaurant dramatically increased, the intensity of my dialogue with Phil dramatically increased as well. This wasn't due to the controversial topics we were discussing though. Rather, it was because the ensuing din from so many people crowding into a small space transformed the concrete-floored establishment into an echo chamber. Thus, as time went by, Phil and I were virtually shouting at each other in order to hear what the other was saying.

If I had momentarily had an out-of-body experience, watching what was transpiring from a lofty position above, I would have grasped the comical nature of this scene. Regrettably, I was too engrossed in my own fears and concerns to even recognize these ludicrous circumstances.

However, any jitters I had from the familiar sound of Phil's voice over the phone were quickly put to rest by his warm, welcoming personality. He proved to be quite interesting: very compassionate, but also very challenging. I believe he could tell I was quite close to whatever new worldview was on the horizon and he seemed to be gently rocking my boat to see if I would shift into a larger perspective of my situation. This shift didn't end up happening during our meeting, but the shift would happen a few days later as a direct result of our having this meeting.

One thing I was grappling with while talking with Phil was the lack of social protest about what was being done to me at the hands of the presbytery. Many Presbyterian ministers supported me privately, but when an opportunity to speak truth to power came their way, a lot of them seemed to duck and run. I understood Martin Luther King Jr.'s disappointment when he was quoted as saying:

"Well, the most pervasive mistake I have made was in believing that because our cause was just, we could be sure that the white ministers of the South, once their Christian consciences were challenged, would rise to our aid. I felt that white ministers would take our cause to the white power structures. I ended up, of course, chastened and disillusioned. As our movement unfolded, and direct appeals were made to white ministers, most folded their hands—and some even took stands *against* us."[22]

Although my participation in civil rights is extremely small in comparison to the epic struggles of the African American people, I, too, found it disillusioning to have so many ministers fold their hands and even clergywomen who said they were advocates for social justice actually turn against me.

126

I relayed this complaint to Phil, bellowing as I did (not due to my frustration but due to the escalating clamor inside the diner), "I just can't see why when some of the ministers see what's happening to me, they don't say something or do something to protest."

"Monica, they are busy people, absorbed in their own lives and ministries. They may want to, but they just don't have the time," Phil yelled back.

"It doesn't take much time to write a letter or make a phone call. I just can't see how when they see such an injustice, they can ethically stay in the system and remain silent, especially when they say they are strong advocates of social justice." I wasn't about to yield my position yet, and voicing these thoughts at the top of my lungs seemed to bolster my confidence in my own opinion.

"I'm so sorry you've experienced so much discrimination and injustice. It can be really challenging for women in the church. I think it's difficult for ministers to know how to protest within the church system when the avenues aren't established. Probably many of them would protest, but they just don't know what to do to help you."

It was clear that although Phil could see my pain, he was trying to get me out of the blame game. I wouldn't budge. I could be a very stubborn Stupid Fool at times.

To appease Phil's efforts on my behalf, however, I decided to let him in on one of my secrets. At roughly just below the level of a mild roar, I informed him, "I know I was called to this situation, though. I understand on some level how to be a catalyst for systemic transformation. Whenever the presbytery or the senior minister does something that I'm critical of, I look for that error in me, and I bring understanding and compassion to that part of me because it's usually rooted in fear."

"Yes!" Phil cried out well above the cacophony in the restaurant.

"Then because I don't believe in actions of pure evil, but only that evil is warped good, I look for the good intention at the very core of their unjust action. These two things clear it both ways." (See pages 169-173 on how to do these spiritual practices.)

"Yes!" he proclaimed even more boisterously, "You've got it! Well, if I'd known of your contemplative interests, I would have brought some Anthony De Mello books. I love to give them out to people. I think you should read his book *Awareness*."[23]

Since I knew God had been using books to speak to me *en masse*, I made a mental note of it for later reference.

During this meeting something else occurred that had taken place a few times in recent months. I had the distinct impression as Phil and I were in deep, loud conversation that I was looking at myself. Not that Phil looked like me, but there was something peculiar in his eyes. I perceived it was my own soul looking back at me through his eyes, as if my soul were looking in a mirror.

This same perception had happened over the past couple of months with clients and in some of the unusual conversations I had that were clearly divinely appointed. It befuddled me. How too was this possible? How could my soul be looking back at itself through someone else's eyes? What was happening to me?

I had for a while been experiencing perceptive abilities when I would look into someone's eyes, especially during in-depth listening to someone as a pastor or spiritual director. I would have impressions as to what was really going on inside them. On occasion I could "see into their soul" with visual images that were metaphors for their inner goings-on.

With one client I had seen a cavernous void inside him with images flashing in my mind's eye of what he used to fill the vast emptiness he felt: food, sex, work. But this "seeing my own soul looking back at me" was an entirely recent phenomenon. I perceived it keenly while Phil and I were hollering across the mustard yellow table at each other. I again seriously considered whether I was coming completely unhinged.

Well, after meeting with Phil, I drove straight to my local library (please support yours) and put a hold on *Awareness*, the book he recommended. I discovered later that the author, Anthony De Mello, now deceased, was a Jesuit priest, a psychologist, and spiritual director from India. His books and spiritual teachings are a unique merging of western and eastern spiritual mystical teaching. And hey, he's funny, too.

A few days later, *Awareness* arrived at the library and I eagerly went and got it. As I was reading it at home while sitting on my bed, a few pages into the book, I thought, *I think this is it! I'm almost there! He's describing my insights, my process!*

Then about half-way through the book, after he strips away everything we have a strong tendency to think we are —name, personal history, reputation, family connections, body, etc.—he then repeated his favorite question for the umpteenth time, *Who are you?* followed by, *Wake up!*

It worked. I actually woke up. I knew who I was. The sudden insight I had sent a reverberant shock throughout my whole body. I was so taken aback, if at that very moment I had also been struck by lightening, I wouldn't have even noticed. After realizing what this new awareness meant, I doubled over, started laughing, and said out loud, "This is the biggest joke in the universe! I finally get it!"

After composing myself, I then got a bit miffed, and thought, *How many people have known this joke and why haven't they let me in on it?*

Then I realized my new awareness was probably not widely held by many people. I thought to myself, *I must be the only Christian in history that thinks this.* I was very wrong about that and was soon to find out.

I turned to look out my bedroom window and saw several birds take off in flight. Finally, my soul was soaring. My grief, the grief that would not go away no matter how many hours, day after day that I wept, the intense pain from all the betrayal and loss that kept me searching had finally fulfilled its purpose. I experienced a profound core spiritual healing through the insight that came from my new awareness. From that point on, my grief was minimal and moments of grieving lasted for only a moment, passing right on through me, and even these episodes became very few and far between. I finally had the big picture that made sense of it all.

I know what I write now borders on heresy. Well, actually, dammit, it is heresy. So shoot me.

I'm joking. There've been enough truth-telling "heretics" executed in church history. Let's leave that medieval behavior in the past. But because I experienced a healing that continues to enrich me every day, I feel compelled to share my awakening insight in the hope that others, too, might experience a rebirth because of it.

The insight, the awareness that suddenly popped into my consciousness was simply this. When for the umpteenth time, Anthony De Mello said, *Wake up.*

Remember who you are. Wake up. Who are you? Wake up!!, a light turned on in my head and I thought to myself, *I am God.*

"Whoa—time out," you may be thinking now.

Fair enough. But before you go and conclude once and for all that my real name is the Rev. Monica McFlake, let me explain that I didn't think I was the totality of God or that I was God and no one else was, like an Egyptian pharaoh. I simply became aware of the divine in me—that my deepest essence was God.

It suddenly all made sense. All of the things I had been seeing and experiencing that had made no sense at all now came rushing together in one, very big picture. I would continue to have many aha's! in the days and weeks to come as new information literally felt like it was being "downloaded" into my brain. This information gave me yet more insights that filled in my new "programming" and rounded out the big picture I could finally see and comprehend. It helped to explain all of the bizarre and wonderful (and even horrible) events that had flooded and overturned my life with the force of a tsunami.

> **The day of my awakening was the day I saw and knew I saw all things in God, and God in all things.**
>
> MECHTHILD OF MAGDEBURG[24]

For example, that's why I could perceive my own soul looking back at me. I was to read a few months later in *Only Love is Real*, "When you look into the eyes of another, any other, and you see your own soul looking back at you, then you will know that you have reached another level of consciousness."[25] This is possible because there is only God, only One Being, One Soul made manifest incarnationally in many forms. "Eventually (you) will see that like a pyramid there is only one soul."[26]

That's why all I could see was unity, why God could speak to me in any way possible at any time through any being. There really is One Mind or One Consciousness interconnected with all (panentheism). I did not believe, though, as some do that all that is in the universe is equivalent to God—that God and we are interchangeable (pantheism).

> "We must remember, too, that the transcendent Being is the only cause, the [parent], and the creator of the universe. That God fills all things not with God's thought only but with God's essence. God's essence is not exhausted in the universe. God is above it and beyond. We may say that only God's powers are in the universe. But while God is above God's powers, God includes them. What they do, God does through them."[27]

Truly a better understanding of the paradox of divine transcendence and imminence than anything I had heard at seminary, as well as a more thorough understanding of "everything is energy."

Finally I could also grasp why the mystics have always said we are each a spark in the divine fire or a wave in the ocean of God. This, too, connected with my new understanding of humans as essentially spiritual, as souls. The divine seed or spark in us also has a layer of "soul" that transcends our bodies, and our lifetimes. It is the part of us that incarnates.

Christ, then, is the incarnational principle of God throughout the universe that Jesus was Master of, but which can and will be realized in all of us in time, through lifetimes of spiritual growth. Christ consciousness is the cosmic web mentioned in the bible: "Christ is in all and through all, and holds all things together."

This fleshed out my understanding of being surrounded by spiritual beings as well. All beings are all a part of the whole, a part of the One. Holographically, we participate in the whole without losing our uniqueness and without losing our interconnectedness. I understood in an intimate way Rumi's (the Sufi poet's) line that God is the dancer and we are the dance. At the ultimate level all is one. God is one even though we experience different beings and levels of God's manifestation or unfolding in the universe.

Shortly after the thought occurred to me that I must be the only Christian in history who has thought, "I am God," I took a walk down to the synchronistic bookstore by my house. As I breezed by the magazine racks in the front of the store, a title caught my eye.

It was a *Psychology Today* magazine advertising an interview inside with M. Scott Peck, a famous psychiatrist who wrote *The Road Less Traveled*. What is not well known about Peck was that shortly after writing his best-selling book, he became a Christian and self-avowed mystic. My curiosity was peaked, and I picked up the magazine and started to read the article.

This is what Peck said in the interview, "I can remember years ago sitting on my bed and suddenly thinking, 'I am God.' And my next thought was that I better not go down to New Milford, Connecticut, (the headquarters of the American Psychiatric Association) and start talking to people about this." [28] !!!

Well, I guess I wasn't the *only* Christian in history to think this after all, even in the past century. Peck went on to say, "Unification with God is the goal of contemplatives."[29] Then I remembered a quote from the German Christian mystic, Meister Eckhart: "The same eye with which I see God is the same eye with which God sees me." Okay, so now there were three of us.

I was to learn there were many, many more.

Much later, I received external confirmation of this new divine awareness in me. At a healer training I went to about three years after the day of my awakening, my training partner looked at me and said, "Oh you have divine consciousness. The vast majority of people do not."

My initial reaction was, *Gasp! I've been trying to hide this from everyone for three years. Crap. How did he find out?*

My next reaction was to calmly ask him, "Umm. How do you know?"

He replied simply, "Oh, I can see it in you."

> **Within the cell of your soul you will find the whole of God**.
>
> ST. CATHERINE OF SIENNA[30]

Now let me state categorically that I didn't know anyone could "see" divine consciousness in someone else or maybe I would have tried to hide it better from him. But realizing that my training partner was a virtual stranger who didn't know me or my story at all, told me that at the very least there was something to his saying this to me. However, I suppose it is possible that he goes around

134

saying this to everyone, but in the intervening time since I first met him I can't actually say that he does.

Now that the secret is out though, I might as well go public with it. Oh well.

Gratefully, the healing I received from awakening to divine consciousness set me free. At the ultimate level, nothing mattered. Not in a fatalistic sense, or an amoralistic sense, but in the understanding that it's all God. God is working out the Divine Unfolding and Reenfolding in Universal Drama. We are just God's bit characters, playing and learning, while we act out the roles we have taken on. But ultimately, God is the author, the actor, the director, the all. Thus, we truly don't have to worry about a thing.

This might be a jarring thought for some, but it was liberating for me. None of the travails, sufferings, and traumas I was experiencing were "real," just temporary diversions from the Real or rather, temporary explorations to lead me to the Real. I realized that ultimately no one could do me any harm. Sure they could take away my job, career, money, house, they could smear me, attack me, even rape me or kill me. But my divine essence was indestructible. They could not touch the deepest part of me. The true "I" could never be harmed.

This is what healed me in the midst of my hell. It made

> **There is no real occasion for tumult, strain, conflict, anxiety, once we have reached the living conviction that God is All. All takes place within God. God alone matters; God alone is.**
>
> EVELYN UNDERHILL[31]

me stronger than anything being thrown my way. At my core level I was one with God, and nothing and no one could ever change that (and the same was true of everyone else too, whether they were aware of it yet or not). All hell had come against me and all heaven had come to my aid. But both hell and heaven together helped me realize who I am, who we all are, and what we and the universe (one song) are here for.

I wrote a lot of poems during this pilgrimage home to my True Center. Here are before and after poems I wrote to capture my thoughts. The first was written when I was trying to put all of my wonderings together. The second was written after I read *Awareness* by Anthony De Mello and woke up.

Before awakening:

metaphors abound

metaphors abound
pictures in miniature
snapshots of the cosmos
God's DNA in all
all is one
each part a cell
every event—telling
a story connected
to everyone
to everything
nothing is lost
all is captured
no details in shadow

all is light
to Thee
though mystery to me
how can it be?
that all I see
is
unity?

After awakening:

just one taste

with one thought
the world is created
one word
the mountain is moved

just one
and the whole pivots on its axis
catalyst
for holy transformation

no delusions of grandeur
no master of illusions
I am who I am
for all taste their divinity

one in solidarity is more than
many in duplicity
one in solitude stands stronger than
the fragmented multitudes

singularity of mind, body and spirit
no one can defeat
a solitary soul
stands alone victorious

God is one
I am one
a taste is all it takes
for you to be one, too

My prayer for you is one taste of Awakening.[32] It will change you forever.

SPoRT

See the Beloved in All

I have on occasion been able to see the Divine Spark in other people. Naturally, this happens at the most inopportune moments, like when I'm in line at the grocery store. I'll be looking around at people and then I'll suddenly and quite literally see a large, white starburst in their inner beings. (Sometimes this is called the core star.) It then becomes immensely difficult to unload my groceries for checkout, talk intelligently to the grocery clerk, and use my debit card without fumbling it around and dropping it. Such mundane things when all around the Beloved is in disguise! On occasions like these I'm left dumbstruck at the sheer awesome and beautiful reality that is veiled behind the holographic mirage of the Universe: God is everywhere.

But most of the time, I have to get into the mindset that God is there—behind every face, façade, and mask. This is

138

a powerful practice that can reduce one to weeping if one is not prepared for the glory that is lurking everywhere and in everyone.

So, at first, only practice this for small amounts of time. Start out with five minutes. For the next five minutes, treat everyone you come in contact with as God in disguise (or the Christ, or the Buddha, or Mary or another sacred name that is meaningful to you). No matter how they look or how they are acting, pretend that you get the biggest joke in the universe, that you can see through the disguise, the mirage, and see God in that person's eyes. I've had some astonishing experiences with this. Once a street person who I looked at in this way suddenly winked back at me with a knowing smile as if they too were in on the joke and knew exactly what I was up to. I had to laugh a belly laugh right there.

Reflect on how this changes your interactions with your family, co-workers, friends, and with strangers. Are you more patient and understanding? Are you more willing to help? Are you able to encourage that person to strengthen their own abilities since you know God is within them?

Of course, this is the most powerful with people who are difficult to get along with. There is a Tibetan saying, "The enemy is our greatest teacher because only the enemy can teach us patience and compassion." Truly, I found this to be true in my saga. Once I found the Beloved (and myself) in my enemies, I could only be humbly grateful.

Increase your time doing this practice until you can sustain it as long as you want and until it becomes a reality in your everyday awareness.

Monica McDowell

$\mathscr{P}$ART THREE:

$\mathscr{S}$EVEN PRINCIPLES OF HEAVEN

Monica McDowell

*N*ow I can hear you saying, "Well Monica, so you woke up to your divine consciousness. This is all fine and good for you, but what in the world *am I* supposed to do? All of these spiritual experiences just happened to you. How can I be on a mystical path if little to nothing like this ever happens to me?"

'Tis true. These spiritual experiences just started happening to me. However, prior to these events, I was already on a path of putting certain spiritual principles into practice. Along the way, I learned some more principles that continue to hold true for me today. Please remember as you read through these that they are principles not laws. Because there are many spiritual principles in the universe, in any given circumstance in your life, two or more principles may be in effect at the same time—meaning one principle may override the others for specific reasons according to the Divine Flow and Order.

However, I've included the seven principles that have been the most significant and consistently applicable in my life. Putting these seven principles into practice is the most direct route I have found to put anyone on the mystical path. There are no short cuts on this path, but some paths are more direct than others.

But no matter what path you take, and whether you end up having mystical experiences or not, we are still all journeying to the same end—to our re-union with the Source. Each person's path is unique. Honor your own path and others' paths as well.

𝒫rinciple #1:

𝒥ntegrate, Integrate, Integrate

𝒮o from the beginning, then. If each of us at our deepest core is a Divine Spark that has become a soul who is traveling through lifetimes and our final purpose is re-union with the One Soul, then what are we doing here?

Finding the answer to this question resolved a smoldering question that kept me in turmoil during my tribulations. I knew that God had wanted me to be the associate pastor of that church. I knew by all the miraculous events leading up to getting the job that I was "called" to that position. There were clues, hints, signs everywhere pointing me, even directing me to accept the church's offer to be a minister in their midst.

But if God did want me to take that job that meant God wanted me to be in a situation God knew would be highly abusive and destructive to my family and me. I could not reconcile these two things. I couldn't deny that God had wanted me at that church. But I also couldn't resolve ethically how God would allow and even direct me into such a horrific experience. That would make God complicitous with abuse even if God hadn't caused the abuse. Like Job of the bible, from the perspective of my old worldview, the only options were either 1) God was guilty of setting me up, or 2) I was missing something.

As usual, I was missing something, as the biblical Job ended up discovering, too. The larger picture that helped me enormously was my new understanding that I was a

145

pre-existent soul that had chosen to experience this hellish set of experiences in this lifetime. My soul made these decisions so that I could learn the Christ path—following the call of God no matter the cost in order to take on a piece of the world's suffering and injustice in the hope of transforming it along with one's self. Admittedly, the Christ path is a rather intensive, crash course in spiritual development, which I can in all honesty see myself eagerly signing up for in heaven, forgetting how much pain can come on earth. Sounds like something my soul would do.

> **The way of the cross is the old way to enlightenment, and until recently it was the only way. But don't dismiss it or underestimate its efficacy. It still works.**
>
> ECKHART TOLLE
> *PRACTICING THE POWER OF NOW*[33]

Since becoming aware that my soul chose this path, I have had a heart-to-heart with my soul and said a few choice words to my soul. Nevertheless, this new understanding has resolved the irreconcilable dilemma I previously had. God didn't set me up. My soul did! At least this, then, was not abuse by God. It was a choice my soul made. It certainly wasn't something I, "Monica consciousness," would ever have chosen. Who would? I wanted to walk away so many times, but I was blocked every time.

Apparently, this soul contract of mine had hefty implications. So my soul had set it up so I could not easily leave the bounds of the contract without having to consciously violate the divine guidance and protection I received on a daily basis. My soul had contracted with God to do this, and God was fulfilling God's end of the sacred deal by providing me with everything and everyone I needed to stay in the game and fulfill my end of the agreement.

Through it I have learned to trust that my soul knew what it was doing. My soul knew I needed to learn certain lessons and it believed this little whistle-blowing escapade would be the best way to do so, and God allowed my soul to work out its choices. I'm pretty darn sure a large part of this also had to do with my needing to balance the karma from past lives I had with this senior minister. There was some seriously bad juju going on between us and it was necessary for me to learn how to release myself from his tentacle-like grip on me.

So that, my compadres, is how I stumbled onto this first spiritual principle. Why are we here? Quite simply we're here to learn spiritual lessons. It helps to see this journey on earth as being in school. Some of the lessons are thrilling, some are boring, some are excruciatingly difficult, even tortuous, but everything we experience here is helping us learn a lesson our soul needs to learn on its progress back to the Divine One. Our soul has chosen the general outline and sometimes orchestrated the specific events and people we will need to encounter in order to fulfill our soul program for this lifetime.

Ultimately, then, everything is for our benefit. I know it is the worst thing to suggest to someone who is in the middle of a painful lesson—this is for your good, really, just buck up. Truly this kind of platitude does not work. What does work is to offer compassion.

So, if you are in the midst of your own hell, I am not going to tell you to buck up. I am going to tell you that what you are going through is shit, and although it is true

147

that shit makes great compost, that is not what you want or need to hear when all hell is breaking loose against you. I know. I've had my heart torn out a few times over and stomped on by forces and circumstances completely out of my control. What this did for my heart was helped to tenderize it towards others going through their own hells. So, whether you are suffering an agonizing loss of a loved one, or facing an injustice that has knocked you beyond your coping abilities, or dealing with addictions, or trying to make sense of a violent crime that has victimized you, your pain deserves to be acknowledged and heard by a compassionate soul.

Find a therapist, a spiritual director, a wise friend or reputable religious leader who can listen to you. Now is not the time for platitudes or principles. It's the time to heal the wounds so that you are whole enough to carry on with your journey. There are resources in the back of this book to help you find someone you can trust to help carry your burden.

To those of you who are not in the middle of a crisis right now, look back on your most recent crisis. What did you learn from the experience? Did you learn more compassion for others who are going through similar things? Did you learn you had more strength than you thought you had? Did you learn that it was okay to let others take care of you when you were in crisis? Make a list of everything you learned.

Now think of a crisis from several years ago. Make a list of everything you learned from this crisis. Then compare the two lists. Have you grown in what you have learned? Are you learning the same lesson from a different angle? Not only is everything ultimately for our benefit—

to help us learn a necessary soul lesson—everything that comes our way also shows us how far we've come.

There is a saying: if you are upset about everything that happens to you, you are in hell; if you are upset about some of the things that happen to you and grateful for others, you are in purgatory; if you are grateful for everything that happens to you, you are in heaven.

And I might add, you deserve to be sainted. Most of us are not quite totally in heaven, are we? We wrestle, we agonize, or we block things out because we don't want to deal with the pain. But pain is a great teacher. Pain helps us to learn not to repeat the same lessons, and if we experience enough pain we can also discover that we don't need to learn the hard way anymore. We can choose to learn without pain.

What helped me a lot was coming to understand that if my soul had chosen this path of whistleblower for this lifetime, then I was capable of learning the lessons and transcending my circumstances. Not that it made the challenges completely disappear, but it did make them survivable and it helped me learn it was even possible to thrive in the midst of hellish circumstances.

Whatever hell you are in or have been through, you are above it. You are a strong spiritual being who is capable of learning the lessons, transcending your circumstances, and continuing on in your journey.

Understand, though, your lessons are not punishments. You are not being judged. You are learning, healing, and growing at the right pace for you. Trust that your soul and God have co-authored the perfect path for you. It is also a good thing to remember that there are different spiritual lessons for different levels. A person at a beginning level of say, learning to speak one's truth, may have a very different lesson than a person at a deeper level of learning to speak one's truth. At one level we may need to learn to speak our truth no matter the consequences. At yet another level, we may need to learn to discern when to speak our truth and when not to. At yet another level, we may need to learn how to speak our truth without saying a word!

Therefore, we must not judge another person—we do not know what level they may be at. Although we may think what someone is doing in a certain circumstance is absurd, you may be witnessing a very advanced spiritual lesson being learned by a soul that is far beyond your understanding. At the very least, we must have compassion for those who are struggling with what appear to us to be simple lessons. We have all been there, and we have all experienced deep struggles learning our own lessons.

Learning our spiritual lessons is a process of integrating. "To integrate" means to make one, to make whole, and thus to make holy. It is where the word integrity comes from. By putting this integration principle into practice, we are making our heart, mind, and soul one, making our unconscious conscious, integrating all of our fragments, all of our parts:

the shadow parts we'd like to keep hidden and deny even exist in us—the fears, the pain, the lusts, the destructive desires;

the underdeveloped parts of our personalities—for example, if we're thinkers, to develop the feeling parts of ourselves, or vice versa;

and the genius parts of ourselves that we'd just rather project onto someone else so we aren't responsible for becoming the brilliant lights we are.

Each thing that comes our way is giving us an opportunity to do just that. To bring out into the light whatever is in shadow in us so that we can heal and become increasingly whole and holy. We are on a tremendous journey filled with divine adventure. The additional principles that follow will help you discover what your spiritual lessons are and how you can integrate the lessons you were born to learn.

> When you make the two one, and when you make the outside like the inside and above like below; when you make the male and the female as one, then you will enter the (realm) of God.
>
> GOSPEL OF THOMAS

SPoRT

Spiritual Direction and Energy Work

This recreation time is more of a plug for helping you find support for your journey than an actual spiritual exercise. I highly recommend finding a spiritual director or energy healer. For spiritual directors you can go to www.sdiworld.org and use its seek and find guide to find a spiritual director near you. This is an international directory and spiritual directors come in all faiths, stripes, and sizes. Through referrals and in alternative directories, you can find a reputable energy healer.

Energy healing work and spiritual direction are on the same continuum, although energy work is generally faster. You may only need a few energy sessions here and there if you are in relatively good physical health. A spiritual director tends to be a longer-term relationship with someone who will walk with you as you work through your relationship with the Divine and the Big Questions of Life.

Both are valuable and in my estimation, necessary to advancing down the mystical path. Certainly, each person needs to find their own unique path and their own unique way of directly communicating with the Divine, but sometimes we need a little help from a spiritual director who is experienced enough on their own path to help point out the signs to us until we can travel light. Other times, we just need a boost from a spiritual director to help lift us to the next level.

Energy healing work goes beyond physical healing and can help you clear the blocks in your body, emotions, thoughts, beliefs, relationships, past lives, etc. in order to create a greater flow between you and God and your purpose for being on this earth in this life. I have had some phenomenal healers work on me and each seems to have their own angle on it. I have needed a bit of work from different kinds of healers to round out the picture; some focus on the body, some on your chakras, some on your energy, some use light, some use focused thought, some use hands—you get the picture. Just find a reputable one you feel comfortable with and who feels like a match for you. Trust your own gut instincts. I've had to turn away from some gifted healers who didn't resonate with me.

I would also add that medical intuitives are a valuable resource when you are ill and medical doctors don't have any answers. If you can find an alternative healing or complimentary directory, medical intuitives and other healers will probably be in there.

If grief from the loss of a loved one is keeping you from going forward in your life, seeing a psychic medium who is trustworthy can really help heal the pain. Through a gifted medium's work you can come to realize that your loved one is not lost or dead at all, but is still alive and well and looking out for you. There are also gifted frauds in this business so again get referrals and do your homework so as to not get burned. I've listed some in the Resources section that have been tested by Dr. Gary Schwartz, an Ivy-league pedigreed scientist working at the University of Arizona who has tested several mediums with double-blind and triple-blind scientific studies, including Allison DuBois of the television show, *Medium*.

Ask for divine guidance and follow your intuition in looking for support. Spirit will connect you with the right person at the right time.

*P*rinciple #2:

*S*ee Your Life Symbolically

*I*f we are each a part of the whole and the whole functions like a hologram, then like a hologram, the whole is also in each of us. In a hologram, no matter how many times you divide the image, the whole picture can still be seen in the fragments. This seems to confirm scientifically the shamanic and mystical principle of "as above, so below." The macrocosm is in the microcosm just as the micro is in the macro.

What this means is that we can look at any part of the universe and discover a metaphor or picture for the whole. Contemplate your body, an event, anything really, and you will find there a picture, a symbol that gives meaning. Learn to see things symbolically. This will help you discern what lesson the universe and your soul are trying to help you learn.

For example, in the midst of my saga when things were completely out of control, I needed a breather. I drove down to a charming town that sits on the Puget Sound. It hosts a ferry terminal for travelers crossing the Sound to go west to the majestic Olympic Peninsula, so there is plenty of parking for ferrygoers who'd like to park and ride. I took advantage of a parking spot right next to the beach.

It was a furious midwinter tempest. White caps, blustery gusts, the whole stormy seascape. I resonated immediately with this metaphor of my life. As I got out of my car and stood on the sandy beach, the weather felt like an exact picture of how out of control my life was.

So I paid attention to what was happening around me. I contemplated the storm. What did it have to say to me in symbols, metaphors, in pictures? I noticed three things. First, I saw a seagull not very far away from me, wings outstretched, looking like it was flying through the sky. Except it was not moving—moving forward that is. Because the winds were so strong, the soaring gull was not making any progress, giving me the impression it was actually stuck in one place in the sky.

I also noticed a duck floating on the surface of the white-capped waves. I thought, *How stupid for a duck to be out on the water in this weather!* But I noticed that it seemed to be having fun riding the waves. The duck didn't seem the least bit concerned about its fate.

Divers were the third thing I noticed. I had been told that right off the coast of this town is the deepest diving water off shore in the United States. I don't know if this is true, but there is a diving area for people learning how to do deep sea diving and that day, three divers were practicing diving in the midst of the storm. *Why would they be out there in this crazy storm?* I thought. But then I realized as they dove into the water and out of my sight, that deep below the surface it was probably fairly calm and not any different than any other day.

What did these three pictures have to tell me spiritually and symbolically? That riding out storms was easy if you knew how to be still. In fact, you could even soar by being motionless, and if you had the right attitude, riding the waves could be seen as fun and adventurous. Plus, if you knew how to dive deep, the storms were of no more significance than any other time.

Wow. I was helped so much by what I learned by seeing symbolically, I wrote a little ditty about it so I wouldn't forget!

Riding Out Storms

on a stormy day,
I watched a gull
soaring
was it moving or still?

it made no progress
motionless
in the sky
with no sign of any stress

on a stormy day
I watched men dive
swimming
would they stay alive?

they disappeared
beneath the squall
under the sea
with no sign of any gall

on a stormy day
I watched a duck
floating
was it out of luck?

it bobbed and tipped
on a white-capped wave
in the sea
with no sign of being brave

not fighting it
not dodging it
but riding it
to beat it

So, whatever event comes your way, it helps to see it symbolically. Like the gull, duck, and divers in the storm, or the blue jay that helped me to see the trickster fool archetypal metaphor in myself, you can find meaning in everything around you.

Even in your body.

When everything had blown apart back in 2001, I developed a painful bump on the top of my foot. It was so painful I could hardly walk if I put any pressure on my foot at all. Off I went to my podiatrist who told me that the bones had probably rubbed together for a long time even though it wasn't visible and over time, stress built up and caused a spur in the bone to suddenly appear. The only traditional remedy was surgery.

When I contemplated the symbolic significance of this, I realized the spur was a metaphor for the pain in the system of the church. The sexual misconduct by the senior minister that had been hidden and unseen in that church for a long time had finally "come to the surface." Now that it was visible, the only solution was radical spiritual surgery, but the presbytery was resistant to dealing with the issue because of the high cost in time, money, and effort. So they opted for the avoidance route.

Considering that this spur in my foot had happened just at this time was no accident. In understanding the metaphor showing up in my own body, I knew this was a lesson being taught to me. And I got the lesson. The lesson, of course, was compassion. I, too, was reluctant to have surgery on my foot because of the high cost and long recovery time required. So, I could relate to the presbytery's non-intervention. It's human nature to opt for the easy way out rather than to deal with the problem.

It didn't excuse the presbytery. They would still need to learn their lessons. By not opting for surgery on my foot, I was also taking a major risk that it would be more difficult and costly to deal with in the long run. But I had gained another measure of compassion towards a small presbytery that was struggling financially with problems that may have seemed insurmountable. My body had given me a perfect example of how the whole picture can be seen in the part. I wrote a ditty about that too, but I'll spare you!

My body continued to be a metaphor for the whole right up to the end of the story.

After the precedent setting ruling of the Ninth Circuit Court in my favor, establishing civil rights for ministers, the presbytery petitioned for a rehearing of this ruling. They wanted the entire Ninth Circuit Court to review the decision of the three judges who had presided over my appeal. We found out in February 2005, that the Ninth Circuit had turned down the presbytery's petition for a rehearing and so my ruling stood.

My favorite line in the documents actually came from the minority of judges who opposed my ruling and thus had wanted a rehearing. They wrote, and I quote, "Most insidiously, the effects of the [McDowell] regime will be that...churches will have to change their own conduct, rules, and theological doctrine..."[34] Sounds good to me! I'm glad because of this precedent setting ruling of the Ninth Circuit court the church will have to change. That was kind of my point. Treat ministers and other survivors of clergy sexual misconduct with truth, justice, and dignity—please.

Anyway, my attorney and I figured we would get some action on a possible settlement due to the presbytery losing its petition. Indeed, the presbytery's main attorney indicated they were ready to negotiate. But after that we didn't hear much from their end. It was frustrating indeed. I so wanted to be over with it.

In the meantime, in March 2005, I had a dream.

In this dream, a Presbyterian I knew came to me. He said, "Monica, I'm so sorry. I'm so sorry."

His news to me in the dream? I had cancer.

Then I woke up. It was the second time I had had such a dream. The first time had been exactly a year prior. I dreamt I had breast cancer. My fear that the poison in the system would get to me had finally gotten to me. Oddly, though, in the dream the cancer only showed up in an ultrasound, not a typical mammography x-ray. So, based on this dream, I went to the doctor and had an ultrasound done. However, it showed nothing. I was told my insurance would not cover it, but amazingly, it did. Because the ultrasound had not amounted to anything, I mostly put this dream out of my mind.

But the dream recurred in March of 2005.

This time, though, based on the dream I went to the doctor and had an actual mammogram. A day after my mammogram I received a phone call.

"Hello, Monica, this is the Breast Center."

Oh no! I shrieked inside. I didn't quite hear the next thing the nurse said. My heart was beating so loudly it sort of drowned out what was coming out of the earphone.

"Um, what did you say you needed?" I had to ask her to repeat what she said.

"I just need to know where your previous mammography x-rays are. It says here that you've had previous film and I can't locate them."

"Oh, I didn't have a mammography. I had a sonogram a year ago. That was all."

"They didn't do a mammography?"

"No."

"Okay. That's all then."

"That's it? That's all you're calling about?"

"Yes."

I breathed a sigh of relief. I didn't have a suspicious mammogram.

In the meantime, a healer came to Third Place Books. I had perused this healer's book on the shelves in January and wondered to myself, *Now why doesn't he come to Seattle?*

A few weeks later, right after the mammogram callback scare, I walked into Third Place Books to see a big poster board of the front of his book with a note saying the author would be there in a few days for a book signing and group healing session. I knew I had to be there. In his book I had seen he did healer trainings and I wanted to attend one of them.

At the book signing and healing session he held, he indeed announced a healer training would happen in Seattle that fall. Great! In the meantime the breathwork he introduced at the book signing would be the great catalyst for my health's restoration, and the healer training in the fall would inaugurate a new career path for me.

A week later, after his book-signing and healing, I received a letter that made me wish that mailboxes were banned as illegal substances. Believe me, the letters mailboxes can deliver can be as detrimental to one's emotional health as meth is to one's physical health. I received enough emotionally toxic mail in five years to poison a whole stadium full of people. The letter I received on that fateful day read, "Your mammogram was abnormal. If you have not yet responded to the phone call we made to have you schedule another appointment, please do so..."

What? I thought to myself, *The nurse who had called said nothing about an abnormal mammography.* My stomach suddenly felt macraméd in knots. I called the Breast Center immediately.

"I received a letter saying I had an abnormal mammogram, but I didn't receive a phone call."

The woman who answered the phone put me on hold while she checked my file. A few moments later she got back on and said, "The file says you received a phone call."

"Yes, about whether I had a previous mammogram. That was all."

"Oh. That wasn't noted on the chart. Well, when would you like to come in?"

"As soon as possible."

The sterile room in the hospital x-ray room did nothing to keep me calm, even though the nurse was being very kind to me. Too kind, really. Obviously, she was trained to try to keep those of us who are neurotics from overreacting at the slightest sign of bad news.

It didn't work. I ended up panicking inside anyway. For good reason, in my opinion. I had to have several x-rays and a sonogram. To my mind, this was a definite sign of bad news. Very bad news. After being told (again) that they needed to do more x-rays, I suggested mildly to the nurse, while trying to hide my anxiety, "That doesn't sound good."

The too-kind nurse said in a falsetto singsong voice, "Not necessarily."

After finishing that round of x-rays, I was finally called in for a consultation with a doctor.

"Well, here's what we have," he said. I was relieved to have some information, even if it was bad.

"The worst news is that this is Cancer in Duct Situ, which is Level 0 or pre-cancer although we don't call it that anymore. Nothing else showed up. It's also possible this is just a fibro-cystic breakdown. It doesn't look like typical pre-cancer, but it doesn't look like typical fibrocystic cells either. My gut tells me it's fibrocystic, but I like to always be on the safe side. We can do a needle biopsy and tell for sure. Or, you can wait six months and see if there's any change."

I decided for the needle biopsy. I didn't want to have to worry about it for six months and send my already fried nerve endings through another round of inferno. Considering I had two dreams that I had cancer, I decided it wasn't worth the risk of waiting.

In the meantime I was trying to get a hold of Mia, my medical intuitive. I had tried several times since receiving

163

the letter from the Breast Center alerting me to the abnormal mammography. But Mia never returned my phone calls or emails. I knew she most likely would be able to tell me if I had cancer or even cancer energy in me at all. Plus, she had done several readings on me between the previous August and January and since cancer energy is generally obvious, it seemed to me she would have seen it if it were there. Unless, of course, Spirit hadn't wanted me to know and then she would have been prevented from seeing it. (It turned out she was out of town for several weeks.)

Moreover, the healer who had come to Third Place Books and whose breathwork helped me so much, had come in between my first mammogram and my receipt of the anthrax-like letter. He has clairaudience (meaning he can hear intuitive information) so he too could probably have told me whether I had cancer. However, because I didn't find out about the abnormal mammogram until a few days after he came, I had no chance to ask him. It was as if I were being kept from knowing what the outcome was. I had to walk through this possible cancer diagnosis completely in the dark.

With everything that had gone on and was still going on, this situation came close to being the proverbial straw that broke the camel's back. I felt betrayed by God. I believed God had promised me several times that the systemic poison wasn't going to do me in. For my nerve ailments, I had once received a synchronistic scripture saying "your nerves will be strong as steel."

Even the day after finding out I might have cancer the scripture I received via email was this: "I am the God of your gray hair and your old age." Although I was glad I was getting a promise of longevity, I was not happy that I still might have to go through dealing with cancer. I started to read up on it but it was too depressing. Even more unsettling was that the only date the Breast Center had available for the needle biopsy was Good Friday, the day Christians remember Jesus' crucifixion. As one of my friends told me, "God sure has a wicked sense of humor with you."

Indeed.

But the fact that this biopsy was going to happen on Good Friday caused me to consider that perhaps this was again all a test. It prompted me to remember this spiritual principle of seeing a metaphor for the whole in my body and in the events surrounding me. Perhaps, I was being asked to demonstrate on some spiritual level that I was willing to deal with the suspicion of pre-cancer in my body even though there was risk and I couldn't afford it.

The presbytery, on the other hand, had lethal spiritual cancer that was obvious and they hadn't been dealing with it for decades. They also felt the risks and costs were too high. However, if I were to hold them accountable and be a spiritual catalyst for health in their "body," I needed to demonstrate symbolically in my own body, a healthy response to the possibility of cancer. I would need to have that biopsy done. I would need to face the truth in myself that they weren't willing to face in themselves.

Wouldn't you know, while my husband was driving me home from the hospital on Good Friday, less than a half an hour after my biopsy procedure was done, my cell phone rang. It was my civil rights attorney.

> **What we achieve inwardly will change outer reality.**
>
> OTTO RANK

"Monica, I just left a message for you on your home phone. The settlement terms have been agreed to. We'll sign papers on Monday."

Astounding. I go through with the metaphorical test and symbolically demonstrate the spiritual lesson for the presbytery, and the situation immediately releases. The lawsuit would finally be ending and it was scheduled for Monday. Monday was, of course, Easter Monday, the day to celebrate new life after resurrection. Another amazing synchronicity. Also the day I would find out the biopsy results.

Easter Monday came. The news came. "Benign." Truly, a celebration of new life for me. However a phone call from my attorney also came. No settlement yet. The attorneys would be wrangling over language for a few more days. I ended up signing settlement papers four days later, on April Fools' Day of all days, a marvelous metaphor of the blue jay Stupid Fool who inadvertently (and might I add, neurotically) is a catalyst for group transformation.

Whatever events are surrounding you or even going on within your own body, take the time to contemplate what picture, what metaphor it is for the whole of your life. Symbolic meaning is there for you to discover what lesson the Sacred One has for you.

SPoRT

Breathwork

Breathwork is one of the most transformational practices I have experienced. Breath is our primary connection to life. We can survive without food for weeks and we can survive without liquid for a few days, but we can only survive a few minutes without breath. In Hebrew, the word for breath *ruach* also means wind or spirit. To be sure, there is a spiritual connection to our breath.

There are many different types of focused breathwork but all have the same fundamental principle. Focused breathing increases your awareness. Rhythmic breathing does as well but it goes beyond this and increases your body's energies in such a way as to promote greater health. As your energy increases, you become aware of the energy blocks in your body (due to attachment to non-beneficial feelings, thoughts, or beliefs) and the increased energy helps you to release these. It is very holistic.

The simplest form of focused breathwork is what Thich Nhat Hanh and others teach.[35] Simply breathe in and breathe out. With each in breath and out breath pay attention only to the breath. You can also say an affirmation as you are breathing in: "I am safe." As you are breathing out you can say, "I am calm." Though this is very simple it is very effective for practicing mindfulness and bringing your self-awareness into the present moment. Plus, you can practice it anywhere.

I first learned a rhythmic breathwork from a healer that is a form of pranayama yoga. It increased my physical well-being faster than anything else. I use it in my energy healing sessions with people and very simply put, it is powerful.

I would recommend finding a teacher or healer who can guide you in breathwork. Certain yoga instructors are certified to teach various forms of breathwork and there are other schools of transformational breathing that you can find in alternative health directories. There are also CD's that can guide you through a breathwork meditation. Please feel free to visit my website to see the feedback I have received from clients who have experienced this breathwork-based healing process.

www.monicamcdowell.com

Breathe!

$\mathscr{P}$rinciple #3:

$\mathscr{U}$se the Universe as a Mirror

$\mathscr{T}$here is yet another way to discover what lessons Spirit has for you. Essentially, the universe has been programmed to function much like a mirror. Whatever is in our soul is what is reflected back to us. So, to the extent that we are love, peace, joy, and other such divine qualities is what we will experience as we journey through our lives. To the extent that we are functioning from a place of fear, anger, lack, etc., the universe reflects that back to us as well.

Me, I tend to be a worrywart. So, guess what the universe reflects back to me? Stressful situations. (Gee, do you think the five years of hell count?) Then I can see where in me is not yet in perfect peace. Recently, this lesson was reinforced big time.

We had a stressful situation with our finances. This was not a new lesson as there were many times in those five years when we lacked money. For the most part, I have learned to take the financial stuff in stride. I'm pretty calm and measured even when we are at a complete loss as to how we're going to pay the bills, let alone put food on the table. But, this time around, I stressed. I got angry, too. I had had it.

"God," I said presumptiously, "I've learned this lesson. I know you will provide. So, why am I still being tested on this money stuff? I'm tired of it."

As soon as the words were out of my mouth, I realized that if I had learned perfect peace about money issues, another lesson on finances wouldn't faze me in the least. So, clearly I still had some learning to do. It became obvious I needed to learn not just how to survive money difficulties but how to be joyful and thrive in the midst of dire finances.

So, I meditated. I embraced a bigger picture. I let go of the mental and emotional turmoil I was causing myself, and I looked for more lessons I was supposed to learn about money this time around.

> **We meet ourselves time and time again in a thousand disguises on the paths of life.**
>
> CARL JUNG

A couple of days later I was taking my daily walk around my neighborhood and I ran into a healer friend of mine who lives close by but I rarely see. We started talking and she said, "You know, I am just so upset about not having any money. Usually, I'm so calm, but this time, I am so emotional and so angry..."

Although I gave no outer indication of such, inside I was laughing at myself. *How is this possible?* I was thinking. Clearly, a lesson was being mirrored for me. I felt this situation must be an opportunity to show that I knew how to have more compassion towards others in dire financial straits.

A few days later, a friend who had moved out of state called me. She and her husband, too, were in financial trouble. She said, I kid you not, "Usually, I'm so calm about these things. But I was so fearful and upset and I don't know what to do." As I reflected back to her what I could hear needed to be addressed in her—how she needed to let go and let God work through her husband rather than trying to jump in and fix things for him—it became clear that yet again the universe was reflecting back to me an additional lesson I needed to learn in my own situation.

How do you know if you've learned the lesson? By your lack of reaction to the situation. If I had gone through this last financial situation without reaction or frustration, but with calm compassion, even joy in the midst of it, then I would see how far I'd come and know that I had achieved the lesson. The same goes for our negative (even positive) reactions to people. "That person's a showoff!" or even "That person is my idol!"

When you react to someone you show that there is a place in yourself that is ill-at-ease (dis-ease) with whatever you have judged in that person. When you don't react, you show equilibrium, balance, and peace. You show that you have integrated the lesson. This does not mean that anything goes in other people's abusive behaviors. It means that you can use peaceful means to solve difficulties and stay peaceful and detached in and of yourself—even if it means in the end having to take social action and file a civil rights lawsuit like I did.

If you find that you are reacting to a person, the key to healing it is to move away from judging and towards compassionate understanding. When I find anything in someone else that's yucky, I remember to ask, *Where is that in me?* I then take the time to find it in myself and explore why it is in me. The other day, I was really upset at a friend's anger. I felt it was completely unjustified and way overblown for the extent of the situation.

Then I got the synchronistic scripture that night from my devotional email subscription that discussed a story about anger and quoted Jesus saying, "Do not judge or you will be judged. Remove the log from your own eye first so that you can see enough to remove the speck from your neighbor's eye."

Well, that was clear.

So, I rooted around inside my soul, trying to find anger in myself. Yep, I found some. I had been a bit cross recently over minor inconveniences my family members would cause me. In fact, I was way overreacting to them and not dealing with these annoyances by using love and peace.

I then asked myself, *Why was I doing this?*

I realized I was stressed, I was tired, and I wasn't taking enough time for myself. The cumulative effect was coming out in anger toward my loved ones. Therefore, I reminded myself to spend some self-care that day and to try to be more mindful before I responded to family members' concerns. I also gave myself an extra dose of compassion, which of course, enabled me to have compassion for my friend in his anger. Perhaps he, too, was tired and stressed.

When I was ready to talk to my friend, I was able to do so from a place of understanding rather than judgment. I believe this freed him to be able to apologize immediately and admit that he had been stressed out about other things when he overreacted to me. I was grateful the universe had yet again, reflected back to me through my friend another place in me where I could grow more love, peace, and joy.

Sometimes, this universal mirror reflects things back to us magnified to an exponential degree, like a funny mirror you might see at a carnival. Putting aside the fact that I despise those funny mirrors because they seem to amplify the very parts of my body I'd rather not have magnified, this little universal funny mirror trick is very useful for soul transformation. It makes the spiritual lesson we need abundantly obvious by over-amplifying the parts of our souls we would rather not see or deal with.

This can be a difficult thing, though. Sometimes what the universe reflects back to us just doesn't seem fair. It could be that the issue in your soul is from a past life and the universe is

> **Relationship is surely the mirror in which you discover yourself.**
>
> KRISHNAMURTI

reflecting it back to you now in your present life to give you a chance to show that you're different now. You've achieved that lesson—so the karma clears or balances. It could be that the universe is reflecting something back to you magnified to the nth degree because without the amplification you wouldn't be able to see it otherwise.

For example, I was dealing with a predator of a minister and an abundance of institutional predatory energy attacking me. Certainly, not my cup of tea and not, in my estimation, my issue, either. However, predatory energy can be very hidden. It is an energy that we can easily be blind to in ourselves. It is an elusive, cunning energy. Maybe there was only a drop of predatory energy in me. Maybe more. Or maybe it was residual energy in me from a past life. But all the same, the universe was showing it to me and it was showing it to me by magnifying it so gigantic I couldn't miss it.

In view of that, I attempted to heal it in me. I used the same process as I described above for the times I notice something I judge as yucky in someone else. First, I find it inside me, then I seek to understand why it's there, and finally I bring compassion and therefore healing into that place. But I also go one extra. When I am dealing with injustice another layer seems to need to be uncovered.

I learned this when I had a dark night of the soul a few years prior to this whole sexual harassment whistleblower drama. Basically, my shadow erupted into my consciousness with all its force and my soul vomited for three months solid. It was not a pretty picture. I came face to face with my own capacity to do evil. While trying to heal this in me, I made the startling discovery that there is no such thing as pure evil. I came to understand that at the very core of an evil action is a good intention, even if that intention has become warped and twisted beyond recognition.

Thus, when I do the process outlined above for clearing the yucky stuff inside me that I've judged in someone else by bringing compassion to it, if I am dealing with some really dark stuff, I also look for the good intention at the core of the person's action I have deemed unjust or evil. Another way to put it is that I find the light in the darkness. That clears it in me and it clears it in my relationship with the person who did something I judged.

The universe continued to mirror predatory energy back to me to help me. One day I was walking toward the bookstore by my home, when suddenly, two crows began swooping down from the tops of the giant, noble-looking evergreens that lined the street, flying right by my face, cawing all the while. Obviously, I was under attack.

Now at the time, the senior minister, the church, and the presbytery were attacking me and it was at its worst. They were throwing everything they could at me, especially the executive presbyter (the head honcho of the presbytery), who had almost as much to hide as the senior minister. I thought the two of them, the minister and the executive presbyter, were joined at the hip, both needing the truth to go away. Naturally, I was not happy about what they were doing. I was having a hard time finding any understanding or compassion for them and finding anything in me that resembled what they were doing.

Well, the crows kept swooping, and I had to bend and twist to avoid being clawed or pecked. I was hoping no one from the church or presbytery was driving by at the time. I'm sure I looked completely batty to drivers going by. The crows were swooping down from such a great height, drivers passing by would have been prevented by their car roofs from seeing the crows.

Not wanting be attacked anymore that day, I walked home another way. The next day I took the risk of going the usual route. As I progressed toward the location of the previous day's trouble, I saw both of the crows lying on the sidewalk dead. Either cars had hit them or someone else who had been attacked by them had taken them out.

I contemplated what was being reflected back to me. This is the little ditty I wrote for this reflection.

The Birds

two crows today
picked a fight with me
walking away
was simply in vain

"evil birds"
I quickly declared
"the world's gone mad
and I am in pain"

I dodged and ducked
to avoid the beaks
what else could I do?
I looked insane

175

on my return
I was not surprised
to find two dark deaths
beside the lane

they'd done themselves in.
over-zealous
self-protection
is so hard to explain

Eventually, I realized the crows were attacking me as it was the nesting season and they perceived I was a threat to their nest. They were overdoing their self-protection quite a bit, and in the end it did them in. But the intention at the core of their actions was good—to protect. I realized, of course, these two crows represented the minister and the executive presbyter. Their predatory energy that was attacking me was a warped intention to self-protect. But I could understand the desire to self-protect one's nest. I could understand it and have compassion for it.

By discovering the presbytery's good intention at the core of their unjust attacks on me, I was then able to find that same energy in me and heal it. Predatory energy is based in fear. It pursues whatever it thinks it needs when survival is threatened and it will attack aggressively to make sure that its needs are met. The crows provided a helpful magnifying mirror for me so that I could find and therefore heal yet another place in me that was fearful, and that had a tendency to lash out when I was afraid of not getting my own needs met.

Having the universe repeatedly mirror back to me the predatory energy within myself but intensified to boiling point, I was given opportunities galore to heal another part of my own shadow with compassion and forgiveness. It was a small shadow part of me I was blind to and wouldn't have seen without the aid of a magnifying mirror.

Use the mirrored principle to try to understand whatever circumstances aren't making sense in your life so that you can heal in the midst of them. With both the symbolic and the mirrored principles, you can discover the spiritual lessons that will help you integrate and create more wholeness in yourself. These principles have helped me immensely.

SPoRT

Wonder as You Wander Awareness

This practice can be done throughout your day. To get into the "wonder mode" pretend that you are visiting this planet for the first time. Yep. You get to be an alien. As you go through your day, imagine that you are seeing, hearing, and experiencing everything for the first time. The colors, the sounds, the trees, the sky, the food—everything. Look, observe, take it all in with an attitude of awe and astonishment.

You will be amazed at how "high" you can get really fast by just soaking in a purple color in a flower, or by focusing intensely on the taste of drinking orange juice at breakfast, or feeling the incredibly fine texture of a feather.

This means no multi-tasking. I know this little beast seems to be a necessity in this day and age, but try this wonder awareness for awhile and you'll see how much richer your life is. You'll need less "stimulation" from TV, radio, and internet as you learn to relish in the abundance of miracles that surround you all the time. You'll cherish more, need less.

I think this is what children are very good at and why Jesus said we need to become as children to enter the realm of God. We need to wonder as we wander. This practice is one that anyone can do at any time.

Here is a more focused "wonder awareness" practice that can help you see what the universe is mirroring back to you.

> **Imagine contemplating yourself from all the points of view of everyone in the universe. It's God being God through God's creation.**
>
> HOWARD STORM
> *MY DESCENT INTO DEATH*[36]

Pick something from nature: a shell, a stone, a flower, a pinecone, anything you want. Look at it as if for the first time. Turn it over, feel it, sniff it, put it up to your ear, get close enough to see the details. Become one with it.

When you feel like you are "in touch" with this piece of nature, imagine that this object has something to say to you about God and about yourself. What does it tell you? If this object could speak for God, what would it say to you personally?

Are you filled with wonder at the amazing revelation you discovered in this one little piece of nature? Well guess what? Your whole life and the whole of nature are overflowing with small miracles and messages everywhere. Wonder as you wander awareness gets you in touch with Divine Mystery in a tangible way.

$\mathscr{P}$rinciple #4:

$\mathscr{L}$ook for the Blessing in Every Curse

$\mathscr{T}$he most difficult principle for me to learn was to find the blessing in every curse. I tripped over this concept repeatedly as institutional evil threw injustice after injustice in my path.

Thomas Keating, a renowned contemporary Christian contemplative, claims that the worst thing to happen to us, even unmitigated evil, might be the best thing to happen to us.[37] Truly, a shocking claim, but one I have found to be true. Again and again, I was blessed and guided not only through divine grace but also through the institutional evil in the church that came against me. It was astounding to me, but heaven and hell seemingly worked together to guide me on my true path. How could that be?

I believe it took me awhile to grasp the concept that injustice and even evil are always blessings in disguise, because it was so outside the box of my old worldview. Moreover, I didn't want this principle to be true. I wanted to be able to label the things that were done against me in nice, tidy little categories. So, I resisted learning this principle, and so the universe gave me many, many opportunities to finally clue in. Injustice, even evil, blessed me.

If this grates against your sensibilities, that's okay. It grated against mine for a long time. Of course, as I said in Principle #1, you must learn to honor your wound before embracing these principles. You may need much time and

179

distance from your tragedy to be able to do this, so be compassionate and gentle with yourself as you heal and move forward.

Following are some examples showing how I was blessed by injustice and evil with some comments at the end to put it all into perspective. At first, I experienced being blessed in spite of evil. Here's what I mean by that...

When I first appealed my federal case to the Ninth Circuit Court, I could tell it had a big impact. My stomach started swirling as it normally did when I could feel things shifting in the larger system. I called a friend and told my husband as well, "Things are shifting again, I can tell."

A few days later I received an unusually large amount of supportive emails and phone calls in the morning. I could usually expect at least one supportive gesture a day that God would bring me to keep me going through all the muck. However, this one particular morning I received a flurry of phone calls and emails. I definitely noticed the difference and thought, *Uh-oh, what's going to happen now?* I wondered if perhaps the universe was sending me lots of support ahead of time to brace me for the next onslaught of retaliation.

Sure enough. That afternoon, I cautiously walked to the mailbox. I had a foreboding sense something was up and looking through the usual bills I noticed "it." "It" was an envelope from a member of the congregation who was functioning as the senior minister's personal lawyer. I could feel my gut wrench as I opened the envelope to reveal what I was guessing were not so wonderful contents.

As usual my gut was right. Essentially it threatened me with counter-suits if I didn't immediately drop my appeal to the Ninth Circuit Court. My response was not calm.

"Oh no, oh my God, now I'm going to get sued? He can't do that. This is a civil rights issue. Oh my God, oh no!"

As I walked back to my house and neared my office door in the basement, trying hard not to panic or be reduced to another pile of tears, I heard the phone ringing. I ran into my office and picked up the phone.

"Hello?" I said tentatively.

"Monica! It's Dave!" "Dave" was the director of alumni at the university I had attended and a very good friend of my husband and mine.

"Hi Dave!"

"Hey, I just wanted to invite you two to a Gala we're holding at the Westin Ballroom next weekend. Just come and have a great time. It's on me. I just want the two of you to have fun. I've got a whole table reserved."

"Wow! Thank you. You wouldn't know how well timed this is. I just walked in from getting the mail with a threatening letter from you-know-who telling me he's going to sue me if I don't drop my appeal."

"What? Oh no! But don't worry about it, Monica. God'll take care of it. Just come to the Gala and have fun."

"Thanks so much Dave. It means a lot."

I hung up, astonished. I was surrounded by grace. All morning and even immediately after getting this nasty letter, I received an incredible show of support. The rest of the day, I continued to receive an unusual amount of emails and phone calls from people checking in with me, even though they had no idea what I had received in the mail.

Of course, I forwarded the threatening letter to my attorney who dashed off a reply to the presbytery's attorney saying this was yet another example of retaliation against me. In the end, nothing ever came of their threats. A week later I heard a minister say, "Grace outpaces evil." Indeed.

I learned that if grace could anticipate evil and outpace it to the extent that I experienced not only in this particular instance, but time and time again, then evil really had very little power. But this was an instance where I experienced blessing in spite of the injustice being done against me. Evil didn't win. But what about when injustice did win against me? My numerous experiences around this led me to the next insights, which had a profound effect on how I now view "evil."

Upon reflection and over time, I realized that—

—because of all the stress from my situation, I learned how to "ride the waves" of a storm and be peaceful when everything was falling down around me.

—the physical damage to my nerves and internal organs put me on the path of alternative medicine and energy healing, and eventually led me to becoming a healer myself.

—because of the financial destruction, I learned complete dependence on God's care for me and my family.

—through being unjustly fired, formally blacklisted and essentially forced out of the Presbyterian denomination, I discovered a hospitable new spiritual community.

—because of discrimination against women in the church, I founded a women's church called Women's Sanctuary, which provided a welcoming community and spiritual safe haven for other women, many who needed respite from abuses of all kinds in the church.

—by being smeared and lied about by other ministers to an extent that still boggles my mind, I learned who I really was. I learned my true core was indestructible.

—due to the sexual harassment and retaliation, I found my own political voice, my own spiritual backbone, and found that my chicken, Stupid Fool heart was strong, much stronger than I ever knew, because it was listening to God.

I could go on for quite awhile, adding onto this list of how injustice and even evil blessed me. Everything that was done against me helped me. Everything. Learning to find the blessing in every curse actually helped me heal my wounds. I resonated completely with the comment the biblical Joseph made to his half-brothers after their reunion. Although his half-brothers, out of jealousy, had sold Joseph into slavery as a child, he rose to a position of great power in Egypt, and eventually was able to save his brothers from famine. Upon revealing to them who he was when they met serendipitously as adults, he said, "You meant it for harm, but God meant it for good."

> **Now I can see just how vast and comprehensive a blessing this period of 'annihilation' has been. It has stripped me, my psyche, my life, my beliefs, and my work down to their essentials, and in return for the multiple humiliations and deaths I have suffered given me the certainties that illuminate this book.**
>
> ANDREW HARVEY
> *THE DIRECT PATH*[38]

Reframing injustice and evil as blessing may be a challenge. When we come up against unmitigated evil we can find ourselves face to face with an incomprehensible, unfathomable mystery. Who can really explain the Holocaust and other horrific atrocities? However, though we may be at a loss for explaining the depth of our personal and collective sicknesses, I still have found it profoundly transformative to understand that within every evil whether disease, disaster, injustice, great loss, or tragedy, there is a seed of good, a holy seed. As I stated before, there is no such thing as pure evil.

Because all of phenomenal reality is manifested from God's intentions and reality is a unity, therefore God's intentions of love and benefit are within everything. This divine intention, this holy seed is not only within every person, it is also within every event, and this seed has the potential to grow and bring about a greater good. For instance, if a couple loses their beloved child to a terrible unknown disease, those parents, if they can find the courage, might be motivated to establish a charity for research into this disease so that more people might be saved rather than die needlessly. With a tragic war, a country might become more committed to peace. This is the truth that "Shit Makes Great Compost"—the true title for this chapter.

Thus as Thomas Keating suggests, even unmitigated evil can be the best thing to happen to us, because of the phenomenal potential for growth for greater health, greater good, greater soul strength that comes out of it. Evil and tragedy are teachers that use great pain to bring very intensive lessons for our gain. I would never have learned so fast without the pain of the injustices to motivate me to figure out what the bigger picture was. It was a crash-course—an intensive one that my soul chose before I incarnated so I could learn some humdinger of some lessons. But it is no different for you. Your soul chose the general outline of your life. The specifics are a matter of free will, but your soul gives you the opportunity to transform the mundane, the tragic, and even evil into glory.

When we can accept and embrace the evil and tragedy that happens in our lives, and name it as blessing, we are set free. To be sure, we do not accept evil passively as a doormat that is trodden upon. Many of the world's great mystics have also been the world's greatest social reformers: Gandhi to name one, Thich Nhat Hanh to name another. Rather, knowing compassionately that shadow and the unawareness from which shadow comes is in all of us, we accept evil as an opportunity for the greater good for us as individuals and for all.

Thus, it may mean you too will be called to sacred activism in light of your tragedy. It may not. We discern our response on a case-by-case basis with divine guidance to help. Sometimes all you will be called to do is to come to inner peace within yourself through forgiveness and compassion in regards to an injustice done against you. This in and of itself will have a ripple effect that will be transformative for you, your loved ones, and the world. It is up to God to guide us. It is up to us to ask God what our response in each situation needs to be.

It may help you to see that evil is illusory as is this entire worldwide drama. Evil definitely exists on this level of phenomenal reality, just like mountains or grass exist, but in the bigger picture it is passing, temporary, and therefore like a mirage. It is not real in the sense that it is lasting and eternal.

Look, I was destroyed unjustly in many, many past lives. But I'm still alive! I'm in a new body, and I'm fine and better than ever.

Evil cannot win because it is only playing a part in the Divine Drama that we all participate in. The Divine Self

185

dresses up in parts and roles to play that we incarnate with in order to learn. But never make the mistake of thinking evil ever wins, that it is Real with a capital R. You can transcend any evil, any injustice, any tragedy if you understand that Grace more than outpaces evil—Grace works through evil and even in evil to bless you.

It was easy to love God in all that was beautiful. The lessons of deeper knowledge, though, instructed me to embrace God in all things.

ST. FRANCIS OF ASSISI
LOVE POEMS FROM GOD[39]

Of course, as I said earlier, you must learn to honor your wound before you can embrace this principle. I also must add that this principle does not condone, justify, or excuse unjust or evil actions. People are responsible for their actions and will have to learn their lessons in this life or following ones. An unjust action will need to be balanced karmically in the future.

However, seeing the blessing in every curse does provide a bigger picture wherein evil and injustice are nullified. When you know evil does not win in the big picture, it has no destructive power over you. When you understand that this entire world exists only in this level and that at the ultimate level the entire material world (and therefore all tragedy as well) is like a passing drama, you are free to embrace and transcend anything in your life that appears to come against you.

I am extremely grateful for everything that was done against me. It catapulted me onto my true path. It opened me to my truest Self. Look for the blessing in every curse.

It can help you discover the lessons you are here to learn and greatly enrich and deepen your life, even if you have experienced tremendous pain and loss.

SPoRT

Looking for God

This contemplative practice is one of my favorites. (It is traditionally called the examen though I don't like to call it that as it implies "exam.") It has two parts.

First, before going to sleep reflect on where you have seen God's benefit in your life as you look back over the day's events. (The traditional language is to look for God's consolation.) I love asking my children when I tuck them in at night, "Where did you see God's love today?" This is a particularly rewarding exercise when you are going through a tumultuous time as it helps you remember and focus on the beneficial things that happened that you might have missed or forgotten about because of the crisis. On some days during my saga, all I could say is "We're all still alive" or "I got to make (and eat) chocolate chip cookies today." But even these were blessings I would've overlooked except for putting into practice "looking for God."

The second part is to then ask yourself where you didn't feel God in your life in the day's events. Applying the principle of looking for the blessing in every curse, then reflect on what blessing might be hidden in the challenges of your day. (The traditional language is look for God even in the desolation.) When something disastrous (big or small) happens in my day, I might also ask myself: What greater good might come out of this? Or, did this event,

187

even though seemingly "bad," possibly protect me from something worse? For example, a flat tire on my car might have prevented me from being in a car accident down the road or made me miss a meeting for a business deal that was not a good idea in the first place.

You may or may not be able to name the blessing yet, but as you attune your mind to this practice, it will get easier to find the blessings sooner. Even if you are not able to name the blessings in your curses for a long, long time, holding fast to this principle will help strengthen your endurance, knowing that at some time, you will be able to see the consolation in the desolation.

I'd suggest keeping track of your insights in a journal, so it will help you see God's faithfulness to you over time.

$\mathscr{P}$rincipal #5:

$\mathscr{D}$etach from the Drama

$\mathscr{W}$hen you know that what is unseen is Real and what is seen is temporary, when you know that no one is lost, ever, and everyone and everything plays a part in the greater good by the principle of Divine Compost, when you know that you are eternally in God and God in you, then detachment becomes much easier.

Simply put, detachment is the ability to let go. It is to be able to see the drama, to see the up and down of one's own life and others' as well, and yet not be thrown off balance by being pulled into the drama. Practice helps. Practice observing yourself. Become the observer and the observed. It is like going to the cheap seats in the back of your mind and watching your every movement, feeling, action, thought, as though you were watching a character in a movie. Once you have gotten the hang of observing yourself, practice observing others and group dynamics along with yourself at the same time. See if you can see the drama. This brings about mental detachment. When you can see the drama, then you can learn to detach emotionally so you are not pulled into the drama.

Emotional detachment is definitely harder. Most

> **Resistance equals pain.**
>
> **Let go—release the pain.**
>
> MONICA

people can detach enough mentally to observe others and themselves, the ups and downs, the drama. It is much more challenging to keep one's equilibrium in the midst of the drama. There are times, though, when it is crucial to emotionally detach. This is when you are between a rock and a hard place and there is no way to win and nothing you can do to control the situation or the outcome. Then it's a must to let go emotionally.

Letting go in times like these does not necessarily mean walking away from the tough job or the challenge in a relationship, although in the end that may be what it called for. Rather, letting go begins with an internal state of mind. It is the ability as the Zen Masters say, "To do without doing." Walk away from the job in your mind, without actually quitting. Leave the relationship in your mind without moving out or legally separating.

How do you do that you might say? By focusing on your inner being. Let go of the other person's baggage and your employer's garbage. You can't control what anyone else does. The only thing you can change is yourself. Inside. Your attitude. Your state of being. Your awareness. Breathe. Be.

Sometimes, when I have difficulty with this—as I am today—(Gosh, why is it, by the way, that I seem to get tested on what I'm writing about while I'm writing about it? What's that about? Hmm)—I visualize cords between the person or situation I'm dealing with and myself, like phone cords. I then see myself unplug the cords that are attached to the parts of my body that are feeling stressed and plug them up to a bright Light (God, if you will). Then I take new cords from the Light and plug them into the voids in my body left by the old cords. That way, I've unplugged from the person or situation and plugged that person or situation into God, and I've plugged myself back into God as well.[40]

Then when I've detached from the emotional roller coaster of the other person or the crazy-making circumstance I'm in, I'm calm and peaceful enough to discern what I am to do, if anything. Usually, I'm called just to be with the situation without doing anything. Then the situation resolves itself in its own time in its own way. Sometimes divine guidance shows me that I am to do a single step, much smaller than I think could have a positive impact, but I find in the end it is enough. Even less often, I am guided to take a big step, one that I wouldn't have had enough courage to do except that I had already detached from the situation and from the outcome. An illustration...

After the presbytery and I settled out of court, I was informed by a committee that I was required to undergo intensive rehabilitation generally reserved for clergy sex offenders (a little scapegoating never hurt anyone, right?) and that I do so primarily at my own expense. (See pages 25-26 of Part One for a reminder of this event.) I was also given a list of several shocking thou shalt not's and told that if I didn't do the psychological evaluation in ninety days or if I did any of the "thou shalt not's" I would be kicked out of the denomination.

I was aware during this meeting that what everyone was saying seemed so *scripted*, I kept thinking the director of this dramatic scene was going to step in at any moment and say, "Cut!" or "That's a wrap." So, it was clear to me I was already mentally detaching. By this time, I had learned a lot about detaching in general, and I knew how to sit and observe a drama unfolding right in front of me from an outsider's vantage point, even though the drama was directly impacting my own life. I also did a pretty good job of remaining calm and cool during this meeting, so I knew I was staring to put emotional detachment into practice as well, even in the midst of the dramatic sludge of the systemic sickness.

Needless to say, however, their stipulations and thou shalt not's put me between a rock and hard place. The choices they gave me: do what we say or we'll force you out, made it a no-win situation for me. Either I did what they said and lost my voice and my integrity by agreeing to do things that were unjust and unreasonable; or by not agreeing to their demands, I would lose my voice by being forced out of the denomination without any opportunity for defense.

I couldn't quite figure out what to do, so I knew I needed more detachment. Emotionally, I had to detach from all the deception and false statements they wrote about me in the meeting's documents, and I had to detach from the significant injustice that was thrown my way by my colleagues (again). And I needed more mental detachment. I couldn't quite see the blessing in this curse yet, even though I knew it was there. I needed the bigger mental picture that would enable me to detach to the point of seeing what, if anything, I was to do.

One morning soon after this Blessed Meeting, I was wondering, *God, really, what was **that** meeting all about?* An interesting thing happened later that morning on my way to do some errands. After I pulled out of my driveway a car zipped in front of me with this on the license plate frame: "Sometimes the Dragon Wins." I started laughing. I mean how many cars have that on them? (Humor helps a lot in detachment.)

But not only was it amusing, the saying on the license plate frame immediately triggered a memory I had from a year prior when I'd read the last commencement address given by the former president of my seminary. Curiously enough, his address was titled, *There be Dragons*, and in his address he had quoted a saying: "No matter how hard you work, no matter how right you are, *sometimes the dragon wins*."[41] After seeing that exact same phrase on the license plate frame, as soon as I got home from my errands, I dug up the seminary's journal and reread his speech.

Doing so gave me the insight that there was still one more move I had left, even though anyone else might think it was hopelessly over. I could now see the big step I needed to take in order to keep my voice and my integrity amid the presbytery's set-up of forcing me out of the denomination one way or the other. Thus, I wrote my renunciation letter officially ending my relationship with the Presbyterians. In this letter I wrote a summary of what happened with an explanation of my actions, along with a genuine blessing and note of gratitude and forgiveness and sent it to every member of the presbytery.

I could not have done this unless I had first detached. I had to detach from any emotional upheaval caused by their deception and set-up of me. I had to detach from

> **Enlightenment consciously chosen means to relinquish your attachment to past and future and to make the Now the main focus of your life. It means choosing to dwell in the state of presence rather than in time. It means saying yes to what is. You then don't need pain anymore.**
>
> ECKHART TOLLE
> *PRACTICING THE POWER OF NOW*[42]

caring about what anyone else thought about me. I had to detach from the outcome to my career if I left the denomination. I had to detach from the consequences of writing and sending out the renunciation letter. I had to detach from the drama.

Graciously, the universe took care of me in the midst of this. Another denomination hospitably invited me into their fold a few days before I'd even sent out my renunciation letter. Moreover, after sending out the letter, I received apologies from ministers in the presbytery when they'd read my letter and finally had some understanding of what had really gone on.

In systems therapy, the essence of emotional health is that each individual in the system (even if it's a system as small as the two of a married couple or a system as large as a national church denomination) has the freedom to self-define and yet stay connected.[43] It's very easy to self-define and leave. It's also fairly easy to stay connected and lose one's boundaries and sense of self. The challenge is to self-define and stay connected at the same time. This is detachment at the highest level. Be in the system but not of it. It's another one of those spiritual principles that are much easier said than done.

Throughout the entire saga, it had been a challenge for me to stay in the presbytery and denomination. I was continually between a rock and a hard place as they repeatedly tried to squeeze my truth into nothingness. I needed, therefore, to keep self-defining, as I was doing with my civil rights lawsuit and all, but staying in the system in the midst of all the retaliation required a great deal of detachment. But by doing so, I learned a lot until finally the situation had come around and I could leave the system at the right time in the right way.

Everyone's situation is different though. You must listen for divine guidance. You may receive guidance to detach by "doing without doing" for a time until a final decision must be made to quit or stay. Sometimes your guidance may lead you to detach immediately by walking away with no strings attached from an injustice. Other times you will be guided to speak your truth, and detach from the possible consequences there are for being a whistleblower. Occasionally, you may find the Divine will show you that the situation is not yours to correct and you are called to let those who are responsible deal with their own messes. There is no hard and fast rule.

If you are unsure of how to ask and receive divine guidance, this is one tried and true method I use. I put a guidance journal by my bed and then write down one to three open-ended statements to God. "I need guidance about what to do to resolve a conflict at work," or "I need direction learning how to detach from helping other people too much." Then, I wait and watch for any and all guidance that comes my way throughout the next few days. In my journal, I write down what happens, so I can see all the ways I receive guidance and review it to see if there are patterns or consistent ways God communicates with me in my life.

It is important for those of us who have a tendency towards co-dependency to learn that detaching does not mean not caring. Far from it. Detaching, if it is done with compassion and from divine guidance, can be the highest form of love.

This verse sums up a lot about the fine art of detaching from the drama.

Letting Go

To let go doesn't mean to stop caring,
    it means I can't do it for someone else.
To let go is not to cut myself off,
    it's the realization that I don't control another.
To let go is not to enable,
    but to allow learning from natural consequences.
To let go is to admit powerlessness,
    which means the outcome is not in my hands.
To let go is not to try to change or blame another,
    I can only change myself.
To let go is not to care for, but to care about.
To let go is not to fix, but to be supportive.
To let go is not to judge,
    but to allow another to be a human being.
To let go is not to be in the middle arranging all the outcomes,
    but to allow others to affect their own outcomes.
To let go is not to be protective,
    it is to permit another to face reality.
To let go is not to deny but to accept.
To let go is not to nag, scold, or argue,
    but to search out my own shortcomings and to correct
    them.
To let go is not to adjust everything to my desires
    but to take each day as it comes and to cherish the
    moment.
To let go is not to criticize and regulate anyone,
    but to try to become what I dream I can be.
To let go is not to regret the past
    but to grow and live for the future.
To let go is to fear less and love more. (*author unknown*)

Detach from the drama. Putting this principle into practice, you'll save yourself a lot of unnecessary inner turmoil and create space in your life for more joy, love, and peace.

SPoRT

Detachment Rituals

Spiritual rituals can help a lot when trying to detach. A simple one is to make a prayer piggy bank. Then when worries come up, write them down on pieces of paper and put them in the prayer bank.

Wailing quilts are wonderful things we used in Women's Sanctuary, a contemplative gathering and dinner for women that I started in the mess of everything to provide a safe place for women to gather apart from institutional church politics. As you may know, in Jerusalem, Jews put prayers in the Wailing Wall, a piece of the rebuilt Temple of Solomon. They write their prayers on pieces of paper, roll them up, and stick them in little crevices in the Wall.

So, we decided we would make our own version. One of the women designed hanging quilts with different pictures and patterns—mine is a lightening storm over water. We even had a tailor who is a Holocaust survivor stitch them for us. Pockets were crafted ingeniously into the design (mine are in the waves of the water) and we put written prayers into the pockets during our gatherings. The design of the storm on mine reminds me of detaching by going deep below the stormy surface waters to the calm at the bottom of the sea.

Find something creative and calming and even fun for learning to detach from the drama. Remember humor helps. The book *Shamanic Christianity* is loaded with excellent ideas.[44] Don't get too serious about it! As those wise Zen Masters also say, "To detach in one's detachment is true enlightenment!"

*P*rinciple #6:

*S*eek First the Realm of God

*T*his principle, my friends, is what I consider the so-called key to the kingdom. Surrender is a very direct path, but it is not a short cut by any means. In sum, it is the ability to say to God, "*Thy* will be done." In Alcoholics Anonymous and other twelve-step spiritual processes this is "giving your life and will over to your Higher Power, however you define Higher Power." I have often preached that the highest calling for anyone is to be able to say, "I'll do whatever God wants."

For some people attempting to say this is terrifying. This is because we have so many non-beneficial images of God stuck in our heads, whether it's from childhood, or difficult experiences with religious misuse of power, or narrow definitions of God that serve human institutions but are far from accurate. We must first recognize that Love is God's only intention and as the scriptures say, perfect love casts out all fear. If we know the Love that is God's Divine Dance in all then we know that God only has our highest and best in mind.

We must also realize that whatever non-beneficial images of God we have, whether it is a punitive judge or a distant, unloving Parent figure, or_____(you fill in the blank), they are false. God is beyond all names, images, labels, even all language. God is the infinite, the ultimate. God cannot be boxed in religious dogma or reduced to psychological dramas. "I am that I am" is the Hebrew meaning of God, in other words, God is indefinable. We can have experiences of God, we can have communion with Love, but ultimately we must say God is Mystery.

In the midst of my tumultuous story, I too found myself struggling with a non-beneficial exclusively male image of God, even though in seminary as a pregnant mom I had embraced the idea of the Sacred Feminine and God as Divine Mother. While at seminary I had even bought and wore a sweatshirt during Christmastide that had a traditional nativity scene displayed on the front—with a bit of a twist. Someone in the nativity scene is pronouncing loudly, "It's a girl!" This sweatshirt has met with laughs, scoffs, astonishment, as well as deep appreciation as I have continued to wear it over the years.

But in the midst of my whistle-blowing years, I was continually running into patriarchy in the church and the good ol' boys club (with even some social justice clergywomen playing into that club) that to an extent, my faith faltered. On one particular day in the midst of the saga, I lamented to God:

Why did the Christ figure in Western history come as a male? I know he obliterated social taboos and stood with women in solidarity in a way a woman in that society 2000 years ago could never have even had the opportunity of doing. I know he is the embodiment of both masculine and feminine attributes and incarnated the Divine Wisdom—the Sophia of God. But why aren't there any women Christ figures? Or even women mystics that are deep in our psyche the way Jesus and other "male saviors" are?

I was really wrestling with this one. It seemed a lot of suffering had impacted so many for such a long time because of this imbalance in our view of a divine man rather than the complementary energy of divine man and divine woman.

That night, unable to fall asleep lying down because of the damage to my nerve endings, I went to sleep sitting up on the sofa in my basement spiritual direction office. I don't know why but many things happened on that sofa in that office. Early in the morning, just after dawn, sleeping soundly, I awoke as I felt myself pulled out of my body just to the side of the sofa. Whatever was pulled out of my body, the "me of my soul," became pure electric. I felt myself held in strong arms and gently rocked back and forth for a little while and then I was put back in my body. As soon as I was back in my body, I opened my eyes and saw a black woman waving at me from the door of my office, and then she turned and disappeared.

Intuitively, I felt she was a black female Christ coming in response to my heart-deep struggle to understand God's seeming allowance of predominantly male figures as divinity in the West. A couple of weeks later I was reading something by Sue Monk Kidd. She stated that more and more people are reporting the appearances of black Madonnas. To me it was essentially one and the same, a black female Christ or a black Madonna. I took the visitation as God's answer to my prayer: even though the West has associated the Divinity with maleness God can take any form she or he chooses to make the sacred real and meaningful to us at any time in any way.

So allow God to open your horizons about who God really is. Allow God to shatter your old forms and images that no longer serve Love or your highest and best. Take a step of faith to trust in the God who is pure Unconditional Love for all.

...and All These Things Shall Be Added to You as Well.

This is the rest of the quote. Seek first the realm of God— [Thy will be done. Pursue the principles of God: love, compassion, understanding, self-awareness, truth, generosity, peace, and justice above all else. Seek the greater good, the highest and best for everyone]—and all these things shall be added to you as well.

What things? you may be thinking.

This quote comes from one of Jesus' teachings. The teaching begins, "Do not worry about your life, about what you will eat, what you will wear, where you will sleep. God, your spiritual Parent knows you need these things." The teaching ends, "But seek first the realm of God and all these things (food, clothing, shelter) will be added to you as well."

> **Live according to your highest light and more light will be given.**
>
> PEACE PILGRIM

Our first priority is to become one with the Divine Flow and Order by putting into practice God's principles and God's guidance for our lives, then amazingly, God will provide for our needs (not necessarily our wants). Trust. Take a small step of faith to see that this is how it works. Much easier said than done. I know. I've been tested on it many, many times. For in all of the losses my husband and I suffered over the five years of hell, financial losses were a big one. It was right after we signed a contract on a house with a nice mortgage that everything at my job blew up around my supervisor's sexual misconduct. Within a few months of that, my husband and I both lost our jobs and my husband's new job paid him only half of his previous salary. Thus, our income dropped by two-thirds. With that and a costly civil rights litigation soon to begin, we were in the red nearly every month. Somehow, we got through. Somehow, meaning, God provided again and again, sometimes miraculously to get us through.

The incident I like the most was during a time in 2003 when I was trying desperately to get our house re-mortgaged with a better finance rate. For the first few months of 2003 I tried to refinance through several companies. Odd things kept happening that would nix the refinance before it went through. For example, one appraiser appraised our cottage Tudor as significantly below what we paid for it two years earlier even though we were in a booming Seattle market with prices going up every year and we had a desirable old charmer on three-quarter acres.

One day when Tony was out-of-state on business, I received a fax. At the top of the fax, I saw the title of a mortgage company I had never heard of and in big bold black letters the fax read simply, "REFINANCE NOW!" I thought this was highly unusual. I mean have you ever received junk fax mail before? I hadn't and I haven't since then either. I decided to check the company out and went to their website. Again, very strangely, the website was not "up" yet and didn't work. I thought, *How weird for a company to fax out information when they don't even have a working website. How did they get our fax number anyway, since it's unlisted?*

Then I got a clue. *Oh, maybe God's in this and is trying to get my attention through a fax of all things.* So, I tuned in and said to God, "Okay God, I got it. You may be trying to get my attention here, but I've tried and tried to get this house refinanced and I can't seem to get it done. If you want us to refinance, it's going to have to come to me."

Then I decided I'd better be paying attention to whatever might happen.

The very next day I received a phone call. The woman identified herself as from a mortgage company in Indiana, saying, "I'm calling you to let you know you've been selected because of your good credit to receive a refinance through us. Would you like to talk to one of our financial agents about this?"

Now my first impulse was to say, as I normally would to such a thing, "No thank you," and then gently hang up. But the so-called junk fax had put me on alert, and so after stopping myself from saying no, I instead said, "Sure."

In a matter of minutes I was approved for a refinance. When they asked me what I did for a living I said, "Clergy."

The response on the other end of the phone? "Oh that's great! We're a Christian refinancing agency." She continued, "We'll be in touch with you about every other day to make sure the process is going smoothly and to answer any ongoing questions you might have. We should have the refinance done in three weeks."

Sure enough, what they said would happen, happened. The appraiser loved our house and though he couldn't find any comps as we had a unique house and property for the area, when he winked at me with a sparkle in his eye I knew it was all going to work out. (Later I tried to track him down for another appraisal we needed done, but his phone number didn't work.) Moreover, the refinancing company called us regularly just as they said they would (shock!) and our refinance was done in three short weeks. This miraculous refinancing enabled us to make it through 2003 along with a new job for my husband.

I later told a minister friend about this. He said simply, "You received a fax from God."

I do believe I did.

There were so many incidents like this—of surprising events happening just when it looked like financially we would collapse. But of course, it never quite happened how we thought it would happen or how we wanted it to happen. This is another part of "seeking God's realm first and all your needs will come to you." You have to detach, let go, and let the universe take care of the details, even if the outcome isn't exactly how you would like it to be.

For example...

On one occasion of being without money, I asked God for some help. The last thing I expected happened. Our sewer line backed up and flooded my basement office. How did this help, you ask? Well, amazingly we got a lot of insurance money fast that more than covered the damage and the unpaid bills I had at the time. God certainly took care of things—not exactly ideal, but hey, it worked.

In yet another situation, we needed to make a financial decision about someone who owed us a considerable amount of money from many years prior. My husband was not terribly pleased with what I felt was God's direction to us to "forgive as you have been forgiven."

After another round of discussion on this topic, I told him, "I understand your frustration. I'll pray again and see what guidance I get."

Off I went to Third Place Books to sit and ponder and hopefully receive some more synchronistic guidance there as I had so many times before. I sat down on my favorite bench where more guidance had come to me than any other place in the bookstore and started picking up books that seemed to "jump out at me."

Nothing. Nothing I picked up or read seemed to speak to the situation.

As I was perusing yet another promising looking selection that turned out to be uninspiring, I noticed a book on a display shelf out of the corner of my eye. I noticed it and then I went back to looking through my run-of-the-mill selection, when suddenly I heard a "whump." I turned in the direction of the "whump" and saw that the book on the display shelf I had just seen out of the corner of my eye was now on the floor. Just then, a bookstore clerk walked by. I looked at him and said, "Did that book just fall off the shelf?"

"Yes," he remarked, "sometimes the books get a little bored and do a little dance, and we have to put them back on the shelf where they belong."

I laughed and went back to the book in my hands as he picked up the fallen book and gently placed it back on the display shelf from whence it had done its little dance.

But, it happened again. Out of the corner of my eye I saw this same book slowly, gradually, beginning to fall. Just before it hit the ground, I reached out and caught it, as I figured this book was literally "jumping out at me!"

The book opened as I picked it up and my eyes fell on these words, quoting a person who had donated her kidney to a complete stranger, "I trust that what I give away today will be given back tomorrow or when I need it."

That was it. I went home and told my husband what had happened.

"You aren't going to believe this."

"Oh no, now what happened." He had seen enough weird things happen around me to know something was up.

"I went to Third Place Books to get guidance about what to do with the debt owed us and a book fell off the shelf *twice*. When I opened it up my eyes fell on words that essentially said that what we give away today will be given back tomorrow or when we need it. I think it's more confirmation that we're just supposed to forgive the debt and let it be in God's hands."

My husband looked disgruntled, "Ok. I can't believe it. Well, you should know, though, a book fell off the shelf twice here while you were gone and it told me we were supposed to collect the debt a million times over."

I laughed. He knew he had lost. He knew better than to second-guess me on this one.

The very next day my husband received a phone call asking him to start work on a job that would eventually pay us way more than we would have received through collecting on our past-owed debt.

Enough said.

In learning our spiritual lessons, there is no more direct path than learning to give things over to your Higher Power. It is a key spiritual lesson. Seek and follow God's guidance and the universe will take care of you. It takes so much trust, sometimes a frightening leap of faith to give all control, everything in your life over to God. Truly, it is a process. We may think we've put it all in God's hands and then a situation emerges that reveals we're still hangin' on to yet another piece of control. But hey, it's okay. God does have a sense of humor about it all. The next story is an apt demonstration.

During my saga, as I previously mentioned, I was attending a hospitable Presbyterian church in a different presbytery a friend of mine had suggested to me. I had been worshiping there for a while, sometimes guest preaching and teaching and doing some spiritual direction. During that time I had struck up a friendship with a woman who seemed somewhat familiar. She was very friendly and fun. We often sat by each other.

About a year after beginning to attend this church I ventured a bit of a risk and told her a brief outline of my story. She surprised me when she said, "I know just what you're going through. I went through something similar on TV." She didn't elaborate, but a stronger bond was forged between us because of our common experience.

A couple of months later, she apparently decided to risk telling me her story. After church she turned to me and asked me, "Did you ever watch the TV show, *The Love Boat*?"

"Yes."

"Do you remember the character, Julie? She was the..."

"Oh my gosh! You're Julie from *The Love Boat*! I knew you looked familiar. I can't believe it." I started laughing. She did, too. She then went on to tell me her story.

I came home from church that day with a smile on my face and a laugh in my heart. I had been feeling heavy that morning, as it was the period in time when I was feeling disillusioned by a lack of political action on my behalf and Women's Sanctuary had not yet been born.

Truly, I think in order to "get it" people have to have the life experience to understand it. Julie from *The Love Boat* "got it" because she had lived it and indeed, she offered to support me in any way that she could, and she made good on that promise. She made her voice heard on my behalf in addition to other actions she took to make sure I was being taken care of. I am forever appreciative of all the support she gave to me, always just when I needed it. She was definitely another way God supplied my needs in a manner I least expected it. I mean, if God can send me Julie from *The Love Boat* in one circumstance, a twice-falling book in another, and a junk fax in yet another to guide me and to meet my needs, certainly God can send you whatever you need in your circumstances.

The most direct spiritual path, the key to the kingdom, is to seek the realm of God above all else. God will meet your needs, and maybe in ways you least expect it.

SPoRT

Sacred Word Meditation

Another name for sacred word meditation is Centering Prayer, the brainchild of Christian contemplative Thomas Keating. I use the former name because it is more descriptive of what this practice does.

In this meditation, one rests in the Divine Indwelling. Rather than trying to do anything at all, like empty your mind of thoughts, you just rest in God. You may notice you have thoughts, feelings, and sensory perceptions come up, but rather than getting rid of them, you just gently return to a sacred word you have chosen and then rest again in God without attaching to anything. If you notice you are attaching to a thought or image, just again return to the sacred word and the quieting of your soul. I like to use the sacred word, "Beloved," but you can choose any sacred word that is meaningful to you: Love, Joy, Christ, Mary, Buddha, Shiva, etc. It is best to stay with the same sacred word over time.

Keating recommends 20 minutes in the morning and 20 minutes in the evening. I think for beginners this is asking a lot and any meditation is better than none. I also like to have people build success by taking small steps. Perhaps 5 minutes in the morning before the kids get up or 5 minutes during your lunch hour is all you can manage at first. That's great! Build slowly from there. The more you experience success the more you will want to do. In fact, if you skip your sacred word meditation time for a day or two after being consistent for a while, you'll notice you miss it and need it. You'll also wonder how you got along without it!

If you would like more information on this practice, I would recommend any of Thomas Keating's books or contact Contemplative Outreach, where you can find other people who can support you in community in this practice. (See Resources.) Sacred word meditation is a great way to learn to "Be still and know that I am God" and to help your heart, mind, and soul dwell on seeking God's realm above all else.

Principle #7:

I Love Therefore I Am

Seeking first the realm of God may be the most direct path, but the bottom line of all spiritual lessons is Love. Ultimately, everything that happens to us is simply teaching us how to be Love in larger and more inclusive ways. In the end it is all that matters. The scriptures say it best:

> "If I speak in the tongues of humans and of angels, but do not have love, I am a noisy gong or a clanging cymbal. And if I have prophetic powers and understand all mysteries and all knowledge, and if I have all faith, so as to remove mountains, but do not have love, I am as nothing. If I give away all my possessions and if I hand over my body to be burned as a martyr but do not have love, I gain nothing." (I Cor. 13:1-3)

Beliefs, experiences, phenomenal gifts of healing, and knowledge are all meaningless and inconsequential if we are not immersed in the unconditional Love of the Divine. This may seem a bit of a contradictory statement for me to make after outlining all of my new beliefs and explaining the experiences that got me there. But it is not contradictory. These new beliefs and experiences have helped me to move into a greater understanding of Love and a greater immersion into living in that Love.

An aspiring student once asked a yogi, "What religion is best?"

"The one that helps you love more," was the yogi's reply.

So, if any or all of these beliefs of mine don't float your boat, don't jump overboard. Just stay in your own boat and practice Love, for as the scriptures say, "God is Love."

Of course, for some of us, we don't really know what Love is. Or rather, we've forgotten. Maybe we've never experienced the Divine Love or an approximation of it from any human, whether parent, partner or friend in this lifetime. If this is your situation, first off, ask God to help you remember and experience what Love is. We all need to experience more Divine Love so we can live it and give it away. Deep inside you where your divine spark dwells, you know Love and you will recognize it when you experience and see it.

So then, secondly, watch. Watch people who look like they know what unconditional Love is. Hint: they are not the ones committing public displays of affection on the street corner or on TV or on the movie screen. Instead, watch parents playing gently and patiently with their children. Watch an elderly couple who've worn their love together through many difficulties and still hold hands as they walk down the street. Watch a kind nurse or doctor attending to a patient. Go to a Special Olympics event and watch the sort of Love demonstrated there. Just watch.

Then, open your heart to this beauty, to this flood of Love that is all around us if we know where to look. Open your heart to feel the Love you see being demonstrated. If tears begin, this is a good sign your heart is remembering and opening to Love.

When you've started to feel Love, then begin to share it. Even if it is just a trickle of Love. Share it with the harried grocery store clerk by calmly looking her in the eye and saying "Thank you." Share it with a smile to a forlorn looking stranger. Share it with a sincere complement to a coworker. The more you share it, the more you will feel it and the more will come back to you.

The universe may test you here and there to stretch your Love. You may get a very cantankerous customer on the phone who doesn't know the meaning of rationality. You will have a chance with this person to show how much you've grown in Love and maybe spark some Love in his heart as well. You may have the type of person you like the least—who rubs you the wrong way every which way—move right next door to you. How will you show Love? Some of us may steer wrong at this point and think Love is a doormat, unable to speak one's own truth, but this is not Love, this is weakness.

Love is strong. It can speak one's own truth and stand one's own ground so gently, so compassionately, with so much Light that hardness melts away. It may take time, but Love has the time. Love has all the time in the universe. Love is eternal. Love simply is.

Love is also unconditional. I came to understand what this means during my dark night of the soul several years prior to the whistle-blowing saga. As I mentioned before, during this time, my shadow erupted into my consciousness and I became very aware of my own capacity for evil. Within me was the desire and impulse to do great harm to others. Because I became so unmoored internally as to who I was, I was desperate for answers and I prayed incessantly for God to reply. And God did.

213

Visual prayer started to happen. I found I could communicate much more quickly and effectively by offering to God a picture of what I was feeling or needing. Even in prayer, a picture is worth a thousand words. Over time, I found that after offering prayer images to God in my mind's eye, new images that I hadn't created myself would then appear in my mind's eye—images that were answers to my questions; deeply, meaningful images that move me to this day.

One image that came to me was in response to following my own line of logic down the path of actually doing harm. What if I had done the incomprehensible? What if I succumbed to darkness? What would happen to me? Would I be lost forever? An image appeared in my mind, a moving set of images, really, a movie. I was on the top of a precipice surrounded by fog with a door in front of me. There was a forcefield keeping me from going through that door. But I knew I had to go through it. I pushed myself through the forcefield, opened the door, and fell. I fell and fell and fell into the abyss. I watched and felt myself falling. After some time, I noticed I wasn't falling anymore. I was suspended in the darkness, but I wasn't upright. I was suspended as if I were being cradled. I became aware that there were other people there as well. Many other people.

I then asked silently, *Where am I?*

The answer came in an instant. "In the womb of God."

I wept, for I knew then that I could never be lost. Even if I had done the most evil, reprehensible thing I could ever imagine, God would still have me in Her womb. I was still loved and always would be loved—no matter what. I also knew at that moment I would always unconditionally love myself.

Many people keep parts of themselves hidden for "if anyone knew about this part of me, they wouldn't love me." Self-hate and self-disgust at whatever vile thoughts, actions, feelings, or memories exist in that part of them keep them from recognizing the inconsistency

> **God manifests everywhere in everything. We cannot be without God. It's impossible. It's simply impossible.**
>
> THOMAS MERTON

of their argument. It is the nature of Love to love no matter what, so Love can't by its very definition stop loving you because of some part of yourself you think is unlovable. To love is to know everything and still to love.

Know that at the core of you, even the core of what you consider is the vilest in you, is Light. Remember that whatever is in you that you think can't be loved is just a good intention that has become warped, but at its core it is Light. It is never separate from God. You are never separate from God. You are always in God. You are always in Love. And God is always loving you, eternally, totally, without any conditions.

A person who encountered this Love wrote a psalm (a Hebrew song) about it:

Beloved,
You have searched me and known me,
You know when I sit down and when I rise up;
You discern my thoughts from far away.
You search out my path and my lying down,
and are acquainted with all my ways.
Even before a word is on my tongue,
Beloved, you know it completely.

215

You hem me in, behind, and before,
and lay your hand upon me.
Such knowledge is too wonderful for me;
It is so high that I cannot attain it.

If I say, "Surely the darkness shall cover me!
and the light around me become night!"
Even the darkness is not dark to you;
the night is as bright as the day,
for darkness is as light to you.

Where can I go from Your Spirit?
Or where can I flee from Your presence?
If I ascend to heaven, You are there;
If I make my bed in the grave, You are there.
If I take the wings of the morning
and settle at the farthest limits of the sea,
even there Your hand shall lead me,
and Your right hand hold me fast.

I come to the end—I am still with You.
(adapted from Psalm 139)

Like the psalmist, you, too, are fully known and fully loved. You are infinitely valuable and eternally loved. In fact, you are Love. At the deepest core, you have never been anything but Total Unconditional Love. You may have lost touch with it. It may take some time to tap back into it again—to tap into the Source of unending, infinite Love that exists within you and within the entire universe. But it's there for only God is Real and God is Love.

Ultimately it was my greatest lesson: I Love, therefore I Am.

SPoRT

Love Labels

I hope you are familiar with Dr. Masaru Emoto's book, *The Hidden Messages in Water*, or that you are at least aware of what this Japanese scientist discovered. For those not in the know, essentially he discovered the power thought energy has on the health of water. He did years of experiments taking water from various locations and subjecting the water to various stimuli and then freezing the water and photographing the ice crystals it would form. Water, even unhealthy water, that had the words "love" or "thank you" taped to its container, would show much more vibrant and symmetrical crystals than those that did not. On the other hand, water that was subjected to hard rock music or a word like "hate" wouldn't even form crystals when frozen.

So knowing this, write the word "Love" on pieces of paper and tape these Love Labels to your water bottle, and anything else you want. You might want to put one on the bottom of your fruit bowl or your lunch box, since water is a significant part of food. You could tape a Love Label to an ailing (or healthy) plant.

> This movement of love you will find within your own soul, because our will is nothing but love, and its every affection and movement comes from nothing but love.
>
> ST. CATHERINE OF SIENNA[45]

You can also use this same principle and send Love through your hands to anyone you might formally touch, through a handshake or a hug, or casually, with a friendly wave or a hand on a shoulder. You can do this for your own body, too, especially to the site of an injury.

Send Love out to the universe in joy, knowing it is making a difference. You are Love!

St. Therese Prayer

May today there be peace within
May you trust that you are exactly where you are
meant to be
May you not forget the infinite possibilities
May you use those gifts that you have received,
and pass on the Love that has been given to you
May you be content knowing you are a
child of the universe
Let this Presence settle into your bone,
and allow your soul the freedom to sing,
dance, praise, and love.
It is here for every one of us.
(Anonymous)

$\mathscr{A}$cknowledgements

$\mathscr{T}$his is largely an anonymous book. Due to the subject matter, I felt it best not to name most of those connected either to the story itself or to me personally. Thus, for the many for whom I give thanks, I will do so in unidentifiable ways as well, though you know who you are.

To my clergywomen's support group, The Ladies of the Rings: I am forever grateful for your prayers, unabashed support, and ongoing friendships. I couldn't have survived the journey spiritually without you. A twenty-one flash salute to each of you from my ring!

To my spiritual direction peer super-vision group: For your grace-filled wisdom, spot-on perception, and the laughter and Love that flow when we gather. Thank you, thank you, thank you.

To my practice group, the Swans: You have supported the birthing of this book with your enthusiasm and provided invaluable insight into my ongoing process. I'm so grateful for the compassion and Spirit in our group!

To my many breathing friends and healing teachers: What awesome gifts come through you! I wonder if I would be alive today without the abundance of healing I have received from you. Authentic spiritual community is such a rare treasure. I am blessed!

To my attorney: You are the most spiritual and principled lawyer I've ever met, not to mention a downright godsend. Thank you for your dedication to civil rights. I hope I made you proud!

To the women of Women's Sanctuary: Wow! What a grand creative manifestation of the Divine Feminine you all are. I cherish our times together, remembering the richness of our gatherings, rituals, and dinners. Your solidarity with me means the world.

To the individual Presbyterian and United Church of Christ ministers, members, and churches who carried me and sheltered me when I needed sanctuary: May God richly bless your courage for the risks you took standing beside me. You were the Christ to me.

To my clients: Though your identities are anonymous, you are known and remembered in my heart. You have been great teachers to me, and what a great privilege it has been to walk with you in your healing and growth.

To my extended family and friends: Thank you for believing in me and simply believing me when deception, injustice, and the implausible reigned supreme. You are the ground which grew me strong and which held firm when storms threatened to uproot me.

To my beloved husband and children: You are the lights of my life and precious mirrors of the Divine to me. I am grateful beyond words for your understanding, your many hugs and for keeping me laughing. You bring me joy! I love you—no matter what.

To those who serve the Light: including, Jesus-Sophia, my angels, guides, beings of light, friends and relatives on the other side, my animal and nature companions, to one and all, thank you for your continual loving guidance and for surrounding me with such a great cloud of inspiration.

To the Source, the Great Spirit, the One who is in all, and through all, and through Whom all is held: Thank you for Life and the mystery and beauty which have awakened me and awoken in me. Your constant faithfulness and ever-present Love have brought me into Bliss. My all to You, Beloved, my all in all.

𝒜ppendix:
ℛesources and Further Reading

Five Years of Hell

Hamilton, Marci A. *God vs. the Gavel: Religion and the Rule of Law*. New York: Cambridge University Press, 2005.

Zikmund, Barbara Brown, Adair T. Lummis & Patricia Mei Yin Chang. *Clergy Women: An Uphill Calling*. Louisville: Westminster John Knox Press, 1998.

Everything is Energy

Adam. *The Path of the Dream Healer: My Journey through the Miraculous World of Energy Healing*. New York: Dutton, 2006.

Brennan, Barbara Ann. *Hands of Light: A Guide to Healing Through the Human Energy Field*. New York: Bantam Books, 1987.
—*Light Emerging: The Journey of Personal Healing*. New York: Bantam Books, 1993.

Hawkes, Joyce Whiteley. *Cell-Level Healing: The Bridge from Soul to Cell*. New York: Atria Books, 2006.

Schwartz, Gary E. R. with William L. Simon. *The Energy Healing Experiments: Science Reveals our Natural Power to Heal*. New York: Atria Books, 2007.

—*The Living Energy Universe*. Charlottesville, VA: Hampton Roads Pub. Co., 1999.

Sheldrake, Rupert. *The Presence of the Past: Morphic Resonance and the Habits of Nature*. Rochester, Vt: Park Street Press, 1995.

Talbot, Michael. *The Holographic Universe*. New York: HarperCollins, 1991.

Heaven is All Around Us

Angels on Earth. New York, Guideposts.

Beck, Martha. *Expecting Adam*. New York: Times Books, 1999.

Fox, Matthew and Rupert Sheldrake. *The Physics of Angels: Exploring the Realm where Science and Spirit Meet*. San Francisco: Harper San Francisco, 1996.

www.barbarabrennan.com   visualization tapes

www.dreamhealer.com   visualization DVD

We are Spiritual Beings Having Human Experiences

Bowman, Carol. *Children's Past Lives*. New York: Bantam Books, 1997.
—*Return from Heaven*. New York: HarperCollins, 2001.

www.edgarcayce.org

Head, Joseph, and Sylvia Cranston. *Reincarnation: The Phoenix Fire Mystery*. Pasadena, CA: Theosophical University Press, 1994.

Markides, Kyriacos. *The Magus of Strovolos*. Arkana, 1989.
—*Homage to the Sun*, 1992.
—*Fire in the Heart*, Arkana, 1988.
—*Riding with the Lion: In Search of Mystical Christianity*. New York: Penguin 1994.
—*The Mountain of Silence: A Search for Orthodox Spirituality*. New York: Doubleday, 2001.
—*Gifts of the Desert: The Forgotten Path of Christian Spirituality*. New York: Doubleday, 2005.

Peale, Norman Vincent. *The Power of Positive Thinking*. New York: Fawcett Columbine, 1956.

Prophet, Elizabeth Clare. *Reincarnation: The Missing Link in Christianity*. Corwin Springs, MT: Summit University Press, 1997.

Rosen, Steven. *The Reincarnation Controversy*. Badger: Torchlight Publishing, 1997.

Weiss, Brian, M.D. *Same Soul, Many Bodies*. New York: Free Press, 2004.
—*Messages from the Masters*. New York: Warner Books, 2000.
—*Only Love is Real*. New York: Warner Books, 1999.
—*Through Time Into Healing*. New York: Fireside Book, 1992.
—*Many Lives, Many Masters*. New York: Fireside, 1988.

Ask and It is Answered

Merrill, Nan C. *Psalms for Praying: An Invitation to Wholeness*. New York: Continuum, 1996.

Myss, Caroline. *Sacred Contracts*. New York: Harmony Books, 2001.

Northrup, Christine. *Women's Bodies, Women's Wisdom*. New York: Bantam, 1998.

Orloff, Judith. *Positive Energy*. New York: Harmony Books, 2004.

Peterson, Eugene. *The Message*. Colorado Springs: NavPress, 2002.

Reality is a Unity

Schwartz, Gary E. with William L. Simon. *The G.O.D. Experiments*. New York: Atria, 2006.

Talbot, Michael. *The Holographic Universe*. New York: HarperCollins, 1991.

Wilber, Ken. *Integral Spirituality*. Boston: Integral Books, 2006.
—*A Theory of Everything*. Boston: Shambhala, 2001.

Finally Getting the Biggest Joke in the Universe

DeMello, Anthony. *Awareness*. New York: Doubleday, 1990.

Schwartz, Gary E. with William L. Simon. *The G.O.D. Experiments*. New York: Atria, 2006.

Yogananda, Paramahansa. *The Autobiography of a Yogi*. Nevada City, Ca: Crystal Clarity Pub., 1994.

Integrate, Integrate, Integrate

www.sdiworld.org
spiritual directors international

Edward, John. *Crossing Over*. New York: Princess Books, 2001.

Martin, Joel & Romanowski, Patricia. *We Don't Die*. New York: Berkley Books, 1988.
George Anderson's work as a medium

Occhino, MaryRose. *Sign of the Dove*. New York: Berkley, 2006.

Schwartz, Gary E. *The Truth about Medium*.
Charlottesville: Hampton Roads Publishing, 2005.
Documented scientific experiments with noted psychic mediums. See the book for a list of mediums he has researched and go to his website for more he is currently testing. http://veritas.arizona.edu/v_mediums.htm

Van Praagh, James. *Talking to Heaven*. New York: Dutton, 1997.

See Your Life Symbolically

Hanh, Thich Nhat. *Peace is Every Step: The Path of Mindfulness in Everyday Life*. New York: Bantam Books, 1991.
—*Creating True Peace: Ending Violence in Yourself, Your Family, Your Community, and the World*. New York: Free Press, 2003.

Use the Universe as a Mirror

Coelho, Paulo. *The Alchemist*. San Francisco: HarperCollins, 1993.

Find the Blessing in Every Curse

Harvey, Andrew. *The Direct Path*. New York: Broadway Books, 2000.

Tolle, Eckhart. *Practicing the Power of Now*. Novato: New World Library, 1999.

Wink, Walter. *Engaging the Powers: Discernment and Resistance in a World of Domination*. Minneapolis: Fortress Press, 1992.

Detach from the Drama

Keeney, Bradford. *Shamanic Christianity*. Rochester, Vt: Destiny Books, 2006.

Seek First the Realm of God

Carroll, Lenedra. *The Architecture of All Abundance: Creating a Successful Life in the Material World.* Novato: New World Library, 2001.

Kidd, Sue Monk. *The Dance of the Dissident Daughter: A Woman's Journey from Christian Tradition to the Sacred Feminine.* San Francisco: Harper, 1996.

For more information about Contemplative Outreach, Ltd., go to www.centeringprayer.com.

I Love Therefore I Am

Ladinsky, Daniel. *Love Poems from God: Twelve Sacred Voices from the East and West.* New York: Penguin Compass, 2002.

Monica McDowell

𝒆 ndnotes

[1] Rashani, 1991. Used with permission. www.rashani.com.

[2] A 1990 study by the United Methodist Church found that "77.2 percent of clergywomen experienced sexual harassment."
Division of Ordained Ministry, General Board of Higher Education and Ministry, the United Methodist Church, *Women in Ministry*,(1996).
Furthermore, in a survey of women rabbis, 73 percent of those who responded said they had experienced sexual harassment.
Arthur Gross Schaefer, *Rabbi Sexual Misconduct: Crying Out for a Communal Response*, The Reconstructionist: A Journal of Contemporary Jewish Thought and Practice, 1 (2001).
Cross-referenced with Northwest Women's Law Center, Brief of *Amicus Curiae*, 2003,No. 02-35805, pp 19-23.

[3] Hamilton, Marci A. *God vs. the Gavel: Religion and the Rule of Law*. New York: Cambridge University Press, 2005.

[4] Rowling, J.K. *Harry Potter and the Chamber of Secrets*. New York: Scholastic, 1999, p. 328.

[5] Beck, Martha. *Finding Your Own North Star*. New York: Three Rivers Press, 2001.

[6] Schwartz, Gary E. with William L. Simon. *The Energy Healing Experiments: Science Reveals Our Natural Power to Heal*. New York: Atria Books, 2007.

[7] Storm, Howard. *My Descent into Death: A Second Chance at Life*. New York: Doubleday, 2005, p. 70.

[8] Beck, Martha. *Expecting Adam*. New York: Times Books, 1999.

[9] Bowman, Carol. *Children's Past Lives*. New York: Bantam Books, 1997.

[10] Storm, Howard. *My Descent into Death: A Second Chance at Life*. New York: Doubleday, 2005, p. 69.

[11] Peterson, Eugene. *The Message*. Colorado Springs: NavPress, 2002.

[12] Scwhartz, Gary with William Simon. *The G.O.D. Experiments*. New York: Atria Books, a division of Simon & Schuster, 2006, p. 17. Used with permission.

[13] Northrup, Christine. *Women's Bodies, Women's Wisdom*. New York: Bantam, 1998.

[14] Myss, Caroline. *Sacred Contracts*. New York: Harmony Books, 2001.

[15] Janda, J., *Julian: A Play Based on the Life of Julian of Norwich*. Englewood, CO: Pioneer Drama Service, 1984. p. 136.

[16] Eden, Donna. *Energy Medicine*. New York: Tarcher/Putnam, 1998.

[17] Grant, Amy and Wayne Kirkpatrick. "Turn the Titanic Around." *Behind the Eyes*. Myrrh Records. Word Entertainment, 1997.

[18] Tolkien, J.R.R. *The Lord of the Rings*. Pt 3: *The Return of the King*. New York: Ballantine Books, 1955, p. 83.

[19] Wilber, Ken. *A Theory of Everything*. Boston: Shambhala, 2001.

[20] Peale, Norman Vincent. *The Power of Positive Thinking*. New York: Fawcett Columbine, 1996, p. 202.

[21] From *Release: Healing from Wounds of Family, Church and Community* copyright © 1996 by Flora Slosson Wuellner. Used by permission of Upper Room Books, http://www.bookstore.upperroom.org, 1-800-972-0433.

[22] As quoted in *Soul Survivor* by Philip Yancey, New York: Doubleday, 2001, p. 38.

[23] DeMello, Anthony. *Awareness*. New York: Doubleday, 1990.

[24] Woodruff, Sue. *Meditations with Mechtild of Magdeburg*. Rochester, VT: Bear & Co., 1982, p. 163. Used with permission.

[25] Weiss, Brian. *Only Love is Real*. New York: Warner Books, of Grand Central Publishing,1999, p. 63. Used with permission.

[26] Ibid, p. 63. Used with permission.

[27] Ibid, p. 172. Used with permission.

[28] Epstein, Robert. "M. Scott Peck: Wrestling with God." *Psychology Today*, Nov-Dec 2002, p. 68.

[29] Ibid, p. 68.

[30] From *A Life of Total Prayer: Selected Writings of Catherine of Sienna, Upper Room Spiritual Classics, Series 3,* compiled by Keith Beasley-Topliffe, copyright © 1999. Used by permission of Upper Room Books, http://www.bookstore.upperroom.org, 1-800-972-0433.

[31] From *The Soul's Delight: Selected Writings of Evelyn Underhill, Upper Room Spiritual Classics, Series 2,* compiled by Keith Beasley-Topliffe, copyright © 1998. Used by permission of Upper Room Books, http://www.bookstore.upperroom.org, 1800-972-0433.

[32] I was inspired by the words "One Taste" by Ken Wilber. *One Taste*. Boston: Shambhala, 2000.

[33] From the book *Practicing the Power of Now* Copyright © 1999 by Eckhart Tolle, p. 137. Reprinted with permission of New World Library, Novato, CA. www.newworlddlibrary.com

[34] Ninth Circuit Court Ruling Feb. 11, 2005, p. 1700.

[35] Hanh, Thich Nhat. *Peace is Every Step*. New York: Bantam Books, 1991.

[36] Storm, Howard. *My Descent into Death: A Second Chance at Life*. New York: Doubleday, 2005, p. 70.

[37] Keating, Thomas. *Manifesting God*. New York: Lantern Books, 2005, p. 21.

[38] Harvey, Andrew. *The Direct Path*. New York: Broadway Books, 2000, p. 18.

[39] From the Penguin anthology *Love Poems from God,* Copyright © 2002, Daniel Ladinsky. Used with his permission, p. 52.

[40] Thank you my spiritual director and healer friend, Cathy Grytting, and her spiritual director, Sally O'Neil, for this visualization!

[41] Gillespie, Thomas. *There Be Dragons*. The Princeton Seminary Bulletin, Vol XXV, No. 2, 2004. p. 129.

[42] From the book *Practicing the Power of Now* Copyright © 1999 by Eckhart Tolle, p. 137-8. Reprinted with permission of New World Library, Novato, CA. www.newworlddlibrary.com.

[43] This concept is taken from Rabbi Edwin Friedman's book, *Generation to Generation: Family Process in Church and Synagogue*. New York: Guildford Press, 1985.

[44] Keeney, Bradford. *Shamanic Christianity*. Rochester, Vt: Destiny Books, 2006.

[45] From *A Life of Total Prayer: Selected Writings of Catherine of Sienna, Upper Room Spiritual Classics, Series 3,* compiled by Keith Beasley-Topliffe, copyright © 1999. Used by permission of Upper Room Books, http://www.bookstore.upperroom.org, 1-800-972-0433.

ℋbout the Author

Monica McDowell is an ordained minister, spiritual director, energy healer, and writer, and served as a pastor and chaplain for several years. She obtained her Master of Divinity from Princeton Theological Seminary focusing on pastoral care and counseling, and has a B.A. from Seattle Pacific University graduating summa cum laude as co-valedictorian with majors in sociology-anthropology and cross-cultural ministry.

She is the author of *The Girl with a Gift, Confessions of a Mystic Soccer Mom, and You are Light* (published by 6th Books in over 14 countries). You can also find her guest articles on the online magazine, *Thought Catalog.*

Monica was the founding director of Women's Sanctuary, offering inter-spiritual, inter-faith gatherings and retreats for women, and she has the distinction of being the first ordained minister ever granted civil rights in a U.S. federal ruling.

Monica lives with her family in Seattle, the land of prehistoric-sized dandelions.

For more information, visit her website www.MonicaMcDowell.com. She may be contacted at *monica@monicamcdowell.com.*

Monica McDowell